INSPIRE / PLAN / DISCOVER / EXPERIENCE

BALI
AND LOMBOK

BALI
AND LOMBOK

CONTENTS

DISCOVER 6

EXPERIENCE 60

NEED TO KNOW 190

Left: Statue of Ganesha with a flower necklace and
ceremonial offering at Pura Petitenget temple near Seminyak
Previous page: Lagoon in the centre of Candi Dasa
Front cover: The pristine Diamond Beach in Nusa Penida

DISCOVER

Sunrise over Mount Rinjani, Lombok

WELCOME TO
BALI AND
LOMBOK

Sun-kissed beaches lapped by turquoise waves. Treks through the jungle to awe-inspiring temples. A rich heritage of arts and crafts. Whatever your dream trip to Bali and Lombok includes, this DK Eyewitness travel guide is the perfect companion.

1 *Canang Sari* devotional flower offerings, Bali.

2 Mount Batur at sunrise, Bali.

3 Indonesian chicken satay dish.

4 Beach on Lombok with colourful umbrellas.

Nestled within the Indonesian archipelago, these two neighbouring islands have deservedly been proclaimed paradise. Bali's beaches need little introduction, with their soft sand, fish-filled waters and world-renowned surf. The island's interior is just as beguiling. Here, mountains are draped in lush jungle and ancient volcanic calderas now hold shimmering lakes rather than lava. Although it's often overlooked in favour of its western neighbour, Lombok also has a wealth of natural beauty to savour, from the idyllic Gili Islands to the cloud-shrouded Mount Rinjani, an active volcano.

Although only 35 kilometres (22 miles) of sea separates these islands, the cultural distinctions between the predominately Hindu Bali and the largely Islamic Lombok are considerable, and each beckons with its own fascinating traditions, festivals, music, dance, theatre and arts and crafts. Enjoy Bali's sophisticated international restaurants, shopping and nightlife in Seminyak, vegan cafés in Canggu and art museums and holistic healers in Ubud. For a quieter experience, head to the resorts of Senggigi and Kuta in Lombok. On both islands there are plentiful opportunities for bartering in markets or indulging in a relaxing massage at a spa retreat.

This guidebook features easily navigable chapters, full of expert knowledge and insider tips. We've picked out themes and created detailed itineraries and colourful maps to help you plan the perfect trip. Whether you're on a flying visit or an extended adventure, this DK Eyewitness travel guide will ensure you experience the very best these two islands have to offer.

REASONS TO LOVE
BALI AND LOMBOK

A natural landscape blessed with beauty. Markets and menus full of vibrant foods and flavours. A cultural history as rich as it is varied. Here are some of the reasons to love Bali and Lombok.

1 GUNUNG KAWI ROYAL MONUMENTS

Bali's "Valley of the Kings" is one of the prettiest sites on the island. Descend through rice terraces to ancient shrines carved out of rock overlooking the Pakerisan River *(p110).*

NATURE AND WILDLIFE 2

The islands' stunning natural landscapes, including volcanoes, rainforests, lakes, river gorges, rice fields, cliffs and beaches, are home to abundant flora and fauna.

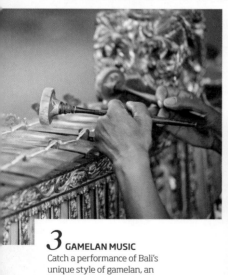

3 GAMELAN MUSIC

Catch a performance of Bali's unique style of gamelan, an Indonesian percussion music played with heavy bronze gongs, bamboo pipes, metallophones, drums, cymbals and flutes.

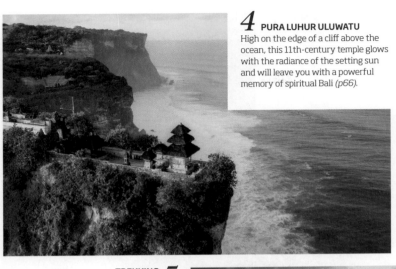

4 PURA LUHUR ULUWATU

High on the edge of a cliff above the ocean, this 11th-century temple glows with the radiance of the setting sun and will leave you with a powerful memory of spiritual Bali *(p66)*.

TREKKING MOUNT BATUR 5

Trekking to the summit of Gunung Batur volcano to see its crater lake and watch the sun rise behind the mighty Gunung Agung is a truly unforgettable experience *(p120)*.

SPAS 6

The wellbeing industry is thriving in Bali and Lombok, offering traditional and modern treatments for mind and body *(p38)*.

SCUBA DIVING IN NUSA PENIDA 7

Attracting divers from all over the world, the clear waters off Nusa Penida teem with marine life, such as gorgeous corals, turtles, silver-tip sharks, manta rays and oceanic sunfish *(p88)*.

LOMBOK'S GILI ISLANDS 8

Did you know there are more than a dozen Gili Islands? Enjoy the famous Trawangan, Meno and Air *(p174)* or relish the seclusion of the "secret" Southwestern Gilis *(p189)*.

9 ART AND CULTURE IN UBUD

Visit Ubud to discover the best of Balinese art and culture, which ranges from dance, music and drama to paintings, carvings and handwoven textiles *(p96)*.

10 TENGANAN BALI AGA VILLAGE

A lifestyle of ritual and ceremony is practised at this enchanting 700-year-old village. Expert artisans use centuries-old skills to create basketware and textiles *(p130)*.

JIMBARAN SEAFOOD FEAST 11

For seafood lovers, Jimbaran Bay is not to be missed. Lining the white-sand beach are dozens of simple stalls serving up the delicious catch of the day *(p82)*.

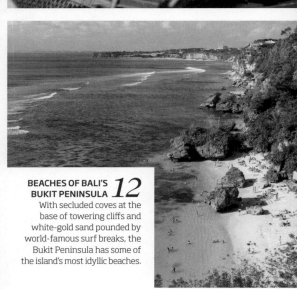

BEACHES OF BALI'S BUKIT PENINSULA 12

With secluded coves at the base of towering cliffs and white-gold sand pounded by world-famous surf breaks, the Bukit Peninsula has some of the island's most idyllic beaches.

EXPLORE BALI AND LOMBOK

This guide divides Bali and Lombok into five colour-coded sightseeing areas, as shown on the map below. Find out more about each area on the following pages.

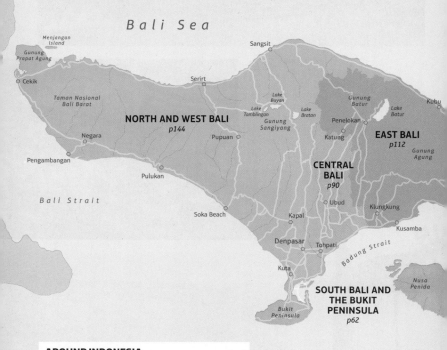

Bali Sea

Menjangan Island
Gunung Prapat Agung
Cekik
Taman Nasional Bali Barat

Sangsit
Serirt

NORTH AND WEST BALI
p144

Lake Buyan
Lake Tamblingan
Gunung Sangiyang
Lake Bratan

Gunung Batur
Penelokan
Lake Batur
Kubu

EAST BALI
p112
Gunung Agung

Negara
Pupuan
Katung

Pengambangan

Pulukan

Bali Strait

CENTRAL BALI
p90

Soka Beach
Kapal
Ubud
Klungkung

Denpasar
Tohpati
Kusamba

Kuta
Badung Strait

SOUTH BALI AND THE BUKIT PENINSULA
p62

Bukit Peninsula
Nusa Penida

AROUND INDONESIA

THAILAND
CAMBODIA
VIETNAM
THE PHILIPPINES
Pacific Ocean

BRUNEI
MALAYSIA

Sumatra
Borneo
Sulawesi
NEW GUINEA

INDONESIA
Ambon

Java
Flores
EAST TIMOR

Bali & Lombok

Indian Ocean

AUSTRALIA

Bali Sea

Kayangan   Anyar

Gili Islands   Senaru

Tanjung   Sembalun

Pemenang   *Danau*
            Segara Anak   *Gunung*
                             Rinjani

Amed   *Taman Nasional Gunung Rinjani*

Senggigi   **LOMBOK**
            p168

Sangsit   *Lombok*
           Strait   Mataram

                       Sweta   Masbagik

                       Praya   *Alas*
                                Strait
Southwestern   Lembar
Gili Islands
                  Penujak   Tangjung Luar

                  Senkol

                            Tanjung Ringgit
           Gerupuk

                            WEST NUSA
                            TENGGARA

Indian   Ocean

0 kilometres   100   N

0 miles   100

GETTING TO KNOW
BALI AND LOMBOK

Two neighbouring islands in the western portion of the Indonesian archipelago, Bali and Lombok are home to beautiful beaches, vibrant towns, endless swatches of paddy fields, soaring mountains and much more besides. Becoming familiar with each region will help when planning your trip.

PAGE 62

SOUTH BALI AND
THE BUKIT PENINSULA

White-sand beaches, secluded bays and a wide range of accommodation options, including lavish hotels and resorts, make South Bali a popular choice. The Bukit Peninsula, with its rugged coastline, clifftop views and watersports, is South Bali's highlight. At the south-western tip of the peninsula is Uluwatu, home to a stunning clifftop temple and beaches famous for their surf breaks. Yet more beautiful nature can be enjoyed on the relatively undeveloped Nusa islands to the east.

Best for
Beaches, watersports, shopping

Home to
Pura Luhur Uluwatu

Experience
Seafood and beautiful sunset views over the sea

PAGE 90

CENTRAL BALI

Traditional arts and crafts communities, water temples, rice terraces, vertical river gorges and lush jungle are what characterize Central Bali. Numerous trails offer the opportunity to witness time-honoured methods of agriculture. The royal town of Ubud, Bali's artistic and cultural hub, is home to a treasure trove of art museums and galleries, a palace, market and monkey forest. Performances of traditional Balinese dance are staged here daily. Be inspired by the creativity all around, trek in beautiful forests or escape to a tranquil retreat for some meditation and yoga.

Best for
Art and culture, yoga

Home to
Ubud, Museum Puri Lukisan, Bali Bird Park

Experience
Watching a traditional dance performance

$\rightarrow$

PAGE 112

EAST BALI

Peaceful East Bali offers a relaxing escape from the hustle and bustle of mainstream tourism, with its quiet beaches and calm, clear waters. This area is home to some of Bali's most significant royal palaces, water gardens and ancient villages. On a clear day, Gunung Agung, Bali's tallest and most sacred volcano, dominates the skyline. To the northeast, set within the crater of a vast and ancient caldera, is Bali's most-climbed volcano, Gunung Batur, overlooking Lake Batur in the spectacularly fertile Kintamani area.

Best for
Snorkelling, diving, rice-field and mountain trekking

Home to
Besakih Temple Complex, Gunung Batur, Pura Ulun Danu Batur, Klungkung, Taman Gili, Tenganan Bali Aga Village

Experience
Seeing the sunrise from the top of Mount Batur

PAGE 144

NORTH AND WEST BALI

With some of the island's most isolated and least-visited areas, this region is characterized by the unspoiled, rugged beauty and impenetrable highlands of the Taman Nasional Bali Barat (West Bali National Park). Further to the east is Bali's mountainous lake district, with spectacular waterfalls, rainforests and lakeside temples. Surfers will be attracted by the black-sand beaches and pummelling waves of the wild west, while divers and nature lovers are drawn to the dolphins and calm waters of the north coast, and the birds and wildlife in the national park.

Best for
Forest-trekking, bird-watching, wildlife-spotting

Home to
Taman Nasional Bali Barat, Singaraja, Pura Meduwe Karang, Pura Taman Ayun

Experience
Dolphin-watching at Lovina

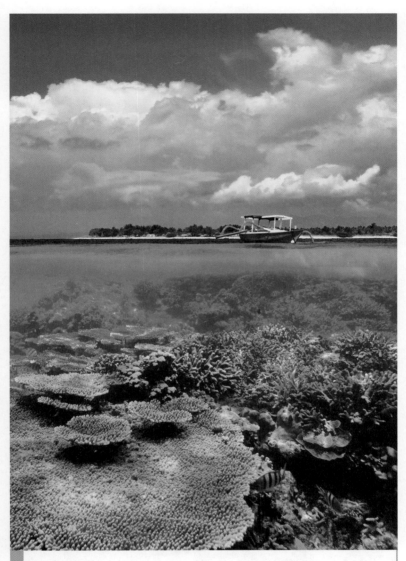

PAGE 168

LOMBOK

Dominated by the mighty Mount Rinjani and bounded by divine beaches, picturesque bays, tiny paradisiacal islands, coral reefs and thrilling surf breaks, Lombok offers a myriad of natural attractions. It is perfect for the adventurous traveller in search of outdoor pursuits, such as surfing some of Indonesia's best waves, trekking the Rinjani National Park or seeking out hidden waterfalls. Divers and party-goers will love the northwest Gili Islands, while the less developed "secret" Southwestern Gili Islands offer a more tranquil getaway.

Best for
Trekking, snorkelling and diving, surfing

Home to
Taman Nasional Gunung Rinjani, Gili Islands

Experience
Bau Nyale Festival, held in February or March

←

1 Rice terraces in the Sidemen Valley.

2 Preparing flower offerings for a temple festival in Tenganan Bali Aga Village.

3 Split entrance gate at Pura Agung Lempuyang Tara Penah.

4 Lotus lagoon in Candi Dasa.

The islands of Bali and Lombok brim with travel possibilities, from short stays in a single spot to great adventures across varied landscapes. These itineraries will help you see the best this beautiful part of the world has to offer.

2 WEEKS

In Bali

Day 1

Start your trip in Sanur *(p74)*, relaxing on the golden-sand beach or trying a new watersport *(www.ripcurlschoolofsurf.com/the-schools/sanur)*, before having lunch at a beachside restaurant. Then, stroll along the paved promenade to the Le Mayeur Museum, the former 1930s home-studio of Belgian artist Adrien Le Mayeur. Round off the day with European-Asian fusion dishes at Kayumanis Seaside Restaurant *(p75)*.

Day 2

Leave Sanur early for the 66 km (41 mile) drive to Candi Dasa *(p138)* via the Sidemen Valley *(p137)*. Stop for breakfast at Komune Resort *(p104)*, overlooking the sparkling black sands of Keramas Beach. Then, continue to Klungkung and visit Taman Gili *(p128)* and the textile market *(p126)*. Pause again for lunch at Warung Organic at Iseh (8 km/5 miles northeast of Sidemen), with a view of Mount Agung. Continue to Candi Dasa, enjoying more glorious views as you descend to the coast. Finish the day with dinner at Warung Lu Putu *(www.luputu.com)*.

Day 3

Begin your day with a hike to Bukit Asah, 2.5 miles/4 km from Candi Dasa. From the hilltop there are wonderful ocean views. Next, continue to the beautiful Virgin Beach (also known as Pasir Putih; *p139*) for lunch at the beachside Virgin Café. After spending the afternoon lazing on the beach have dinner at Watergarden Café *(www.watergardenhotel.com)*, with its menu of international dishes.

Day 4

Trek in the lush countryside around Candi Dasa with a local guide, such as Paleng *(www.palengsbali.com/trekking.html)*. Most tours end at the fascinating Bali Aga village at Tenganan *(p130)*. Return to Candi Dasa for lunch; visit the lotus lagoon, and then enjoy a blissful Balinese Healer treatment at Spa Alila Manggis *(p39)*. Enjoy dinner in the romantic garden of Vincent's Restaurant *(www.vincentsbali.com)*.

Day 5

Drive to Jasri (12 km/5 miles) for a tour of the delightful Sorga Organic Chocolate Factory *(p140)*. Leave room for a gourmet lunch at Bali Asli (8.5 km/5.5 miles north) *(p143)*. Then in the afternoon, marvel at the architecture and stunning gardens of two lavish water palaces, Tirtagangga *(p136)* and Taman Ujung Water Palace *(p139)*. The cheerful Warung Lesehan Mina Carik *(Jalan Ahman Jani, Amlapura)* is a great place for dinner.

Day 6

Drive 21 km (13 miles) to the hilltop temples of Pura Lempuyang *(p140)*. If you don't fancy the climb up the 1,700 steps to the summit, stop at the first temple, Pura Agung Lempuyang Tara Penah, for an awe-inspiring vista of Mount Agung framed by the split gates. Continue to Amed *(p141)* through yet more eye-popping scenery. Spend the afternoon snorkelling around a Japanese shipwreck at Lipah Bay, an easy swim from the shore. Dine on local dishes at Warung Enak *(p141)*.

→

Day 7

Wake up early to see the sunrise over Lombok and the little *jukung* fishing boats returning with the night's catch. Then, trek to the Five Holy Springs just outside Amed with a local guide. After lunch charter a traditional boat and captain for an exploration of the coastline. End the day with dinner at Sails Restaurant *(p141)*.

Day 8

Set out on a leisurely drive through the volcanic landscape along the coast to Lovina (88 km/55 miles) *(p166)*. Stop at the Cili Emas Oceanside Resort in Tejaula for lunch *(www.ciliemas.com)*. At the nearby village of Les, take a short walk through plantations of papaya and pineapple to Yeh Mempeh waterfall *(p167)*. Continue your drive, stopping to see the humorous relief carvings at Pura Dalem Jagaraga temple *(p167)*. Then drive through the streets of Singaraja *(p150)*, the former Dutch capital, to take in its waterfront warehouses. A 20-minute drive from here brings you to Lovina, where your hotel can arrange a morning dolphin-watching tour.

Day 9

Get up at the crack of dawn for your dolphin-watching excursion off Lovina in a traditional boat. Pods of dolphins come out every morning to play in the bay. Then head west to Pemuteran (45 km/28 miles), stopping off en route for a tour of Hatten Wines Vineyards at Sanggalangit *(p163)*. In the afternoon, snorkel or dive among the beautiful coral reefs at Pemuteran. Dine at the beachside Pondok Sari restaurant *(www.pondoksari.com)*.

Day 10

Set out early for Pura Puncak Manik (5 km/3 miles), a beautiful small temple built around a sacred spring high up in the hills. You have to climb hundreds of steps, but when you reach the top, you will be rewarded with a marvellous view. Return to Pemuteran for lunch. Then drive to the Menjangan area (12 km/7.5 miles). Spend the afternoon relaxing at Pasir Putih Beach Club at the luxurious Menjangan Dynasty Resort *(www.mdr.pphotels.com)*, which has bathing pools fed by natural hot springs.

1 Gate in the Pura Taman Ayun royal temple, Mengwi.

2 Grapes in vineyards at Sanggalangit.

3 Dolphin-watching expedition off the coast of Lovina.

4 Colourful beach bar on Seminyak Beach, just north of Kuta.

5 Bali Tower in the Menjangan Resort, overlooking the forest of the West Bali National Park and the landscape beyond.

Day 11

Snorkel or dive around Menjangan Island, famous for its flourishing marine life, lack of currents and crystal-clear waters. In the afternoon, head to the Menjangan Resort (www.themenjangan.com) to arrange a horse-riding excursion through Taman Nasional Bali Barat (West Bali National Park; p149). Later, climb the resort's Bali Tower for a sunset vista of monsoon forest, the East Java mountains, Menjangan Island and the Bali landscape, laid out like a map.

Day 12

Arrange for a national park guide to take you on an easy trek through West Bali National Park for some birdwatching and wildlife spotting. Enjoy lunch at Mimpi Resort Menjangan (p163), followed by an afternoon relaxing in the healing waters of Mimpi's hot-spring bathing pools.

Day 13

Set out on the picturesque 136-km (85-mile) drive to Seminyak (p79). Head east, stopping for a tour of Atlas South Sea Pearl Farm at Penyabangan (p163). Then turn inland at Sererit and drive south through the spectacular scenery of Pupuan for 65 km (41 miles) to Cempaka Belimbing Villas (www.cempakabelimbing.com) for lunch with a view of beautiful rice fields. Continue your journey, turning off the main road at Mengwi to visit the splendid garden-temple of Pura Taman Ayun (p154), followed by another detour after 16 km (10 miles) to the dramatic sea temple of Tanah Lot (p156). Continue to Seminyak. Dine at Mama San (p78).

Day 14

Enjoy a gourmet breakfast at La Lucciola (Jalan Kayu Aya), overlooking the beach. Spend the morning visiting the markets near Seminyak Square. Lunch at Taco Beach Grill (p78). In the afternoon, relax on Seminyak Beach and participate in the daily beach-bar sunset ritual, drinking a beer or a cocktail, while sitting on a bean-bag on the sand listening to live music. Have dinner on Jalan Petitenget, followed by a champagne cocktail at Red Carpet (www.redcarpetchampagnebar.com).

→

1 Kuta Beach, lined with tropical-style resorts.

2 Traditional songket weaving at Sade village.

3 Pura Batu Bolong, on a rock jutting out to sea.

4 Horizon at Ashtari restaurant on a hilltop, Kuta.

10 DAYS

In Lombok and the Gili Islands

Day 1

From Lombok Airport drive south to Kuta (19 km/12 miles), and explore the Kuta Beach area (p186). There is plenty of accommodation here. For a luxurious option, choose the beachfront Novotel Lombok (www.novotellombok.com), 10 minutes' drive east of Kuta. After checking in, drive north (6 km/4 miles from Kuta) to Dusun Sade weaving village, whose shops stock a range of woven fabrics. Head back south to Ashtari Lounge & Kitchen nearby (www.ashtarilombok.com) for a drink; nothing beats the view from here at sunset. If you're feeling active, join a sunset yoga class on the patio. Drive back to Kuta (4 km/2 miles) for dinner at Bush Radio (p186), followed by cocktails at the beachside Surfer's Bar (Jalan Raya Bunutan 1), which has live music on Fridays.

Day 2

Visit Putri Nyale Beach, 15 minutes' drive east of Kuta, a place of beauty and legend and the site of Lombok's famous Bau Nyale festival (p187). At Seger Beach next door is a statue of the legendary Princess Mandalika. A seven-minute drive west will bring you to a roundabout, where you can turn back down to the coast to Mandalika Beach and the Novotel Lombok. Treat yourself to lunch amid the eccentric fairytale architecture of this stylish resort. Drive east to Tanjung Aan Beach (4 km/ 2.5 miles) (p186), where there are reefs just offshore, perfect for snorkelling. Climb Merese Hill for gorgeous sunset views. For dinner, head to KRNK (p186) for pizza, cocktails and tunes.

Day 3

Drive to Mawun Beach (10 km/6 miles west of Kuta; p187). Stop for a swim and, if you'd like to try your hand at surfing, continue another 9 km (5 miles) west to Selong Belanak Beach (p188), where the gentle waves are ideal for beginner surfers. Have lunch at the delightful Laut Biru Bar and Restaurant, which serves up Indonesian classics on a pretty terrace (www.sempiak villas.com/laut-biru-bar-restaurant). Then, charter a boat from the local fishers and try your hand at catching your own seafood. Be sure to be back on dry land in time to watch the buffaloes being herded along the water's edge at sunset. Kampung Café (Jalan Selong Belanak) is a good place for dinner, with its menu of delicious Indonesian and Western dishes.

Day 4

Head 40 km (25 miles) north to the intriguing traditional pottery village of Banyumelek (p189). Tour the galleries to watch artisans at work, then continue 13 km (8 miles) north to Mataram(p178). Stop for lunch here and visit Sekarbela village if you're interested in purchasing some fine-quality pearls. In the afternoon drive 18 km (11 miles) north to Senggigi (p180). You'll pass the Hindu temple of Pura Batu Bolong, which juts out to sea straddling an archway in the rock. Once you've reached your destination, explore Senggigi's beachfront, which is lined with cafés and restaurants. A good dinner option is Square Restaurant (p180). Round off the day with a drink at one of the bars lining the beach.

→

Day 5

Continue north to Bangsal, which is the departure point for the Gili Islands *(p174)*. Take a public ferry to the island nearest to the mainland, Gili Air, explore the island on foot or by bicycle and enjoy lunch at one of the numerous cafés on the beach. Spend the afternoon snorkelling – there's a good chance you'll see a turtle. If you're a diver, don't miss the opportunity to see rare mandarinfish in the harbour at sunset, otherwise head to the west side of the island to watch the sunset to see Bali's Mount Agung silhouetted against a red sky. Have dinner lounging on comfy bean bags overlooking the ocean at Mowie's Bar *(Jalan Gili Air)*.

Day 6

Wake up early to see the sunrise over Lombok's Mount Rinjani. Take a hopper boat to Gili Meno, the smallest and least-developed of the three northwestern Gili islands. Snorkel at Blue Coral Point off the northeast coast, which has a beautiful coral reef, or search for hawksbill or green turtles off the northwestern part of the island.

Jump on a hopper boat to the third and largest island, Gili Trawangan. Spend the afternoon either at a spa or, if you're feeling energetic, go on a guided horse ride around the island with Stud Stables. Dine beside the beach.

Day 7

Take the ferry back to Bangsal on the mainland for your 60-km (37-mile) journey to Senaru, gateway to Taman Nasional Gunung Rinjani national park *(p173)*. Head northeast along the rollercoaster road hugging the dramatic coastline all the way from Senggigi to Anyar, where it drops inland to Bayan. Winding around the palm-fringed bays of Karang, Mangsit, Malimbu, Teluk Kodek, Nippah and Teluk, the road will treat you to fine views of the Gili Islands. At Bayan, thought to be the birthplace of the island's Wetu Telu religion *(p179)*, stop outside Lombok's oldest mosque, a striking tiered building, constructed of bamboo and thatch atop a circular stone platform *(p182)*. Check in to your accommodation at Senaru Rinjani Mountain Lodge *(www.rinjanilodge.com)*,

① Tiu Kelep Waterfall near Senaru.

② Typical street on Gili Trawangan.

③ Lounging on beanbags at Mowie's Bar on Gili Air.

④ Sun setting behind Mount Agung, as seen from Gili Air.

⑤ Spa on Gili Trawangan.

⑥ Snorkelling off Gili Meno.

with its spectacular views of the mountain. Grab a bite to eat in the restaurant there. In the afternoon, take a tour with one of the local women guides of the traditional Sasak village of Dusun Senaru (www.rinjani womenadventure.com/senaru-village-expedition) and its gardens of fruits and spices. This is the oldest traditional village in Lombok, a living museum of grass-roofed, woven-bamboo houses. After dinner, sit on the open-air terrace of the restaurant or your room, and relish the sounds of nature.

Day 8

Wake up early to see the sunrise over Mount Rinjani. With a local guide, descend a well-trodden flight of steps through the tropical forest to Sindang Gila, a roaring 40-m (130-ft) tiered waterfall. Continue your walk alongside an old irrigation canal to the dazzling Tiu Kelep waterfall (p183). Take a dip in the pool beneath the falls and swim behind the main cascade; according to local legend you will emerge one year younger. Move back downstream and soak in the river's jacuzzi-like pools.

In the afternoon drive to Sembalun (p182), which takes approximately two hours through awe-inspiring scenery on wind-ing mountain roads. For an unbeatable experience, check into a home-stay, where you can enjoy home-cooked Sasak mountain cuisine. Unsullied by streetlights, the night sky over Sembalun is truly magnificent.

Day 9

Spend a day hiking with an official guide in the Taman Nasional Gunung Rinjani national park (p173). Not everyone comes here to climb the volcano: other trekking options include the nine-hour Sembalun Wildflowers Walk to see the stunning local flora at the Savana Propok outlook.

Day 10

Depart Sembalun for the three-hour drive back to the airport. Stop en route at Sukarara weaving village, just 12 km (8 miles) from the airport. Here you can buy traditional songket textiles and watch the weavers at work.

←

1 Tegallalang rice terraces.

2 Monkeys and statuary in the Sacred Monkey Forest.

3 Traditional dance at Puri Saren.

4 Craftsman at work in an art studio.

5 DAYS
In Ubud

Day 1

Start with a walk through the Sacred Monkey Forest *(p98)*. Remember to hold on to your hat and sunglasses! Then stroll up Jalan Hanoman *(p99)*, stopping at the charming F.R.E.A.K coffee shop. Turn right at the top and you'll find Ubud market, with great handicrafts. Head west along the main road to the footpath at Abangan Bungalows, and take a 20-minute walk through the lovely rice fields to Sari Organic *(Jalan Subak Sok Waya)* for lunch. After lunch, explore the shops and arrange for a car and driver to take you to Petulu village (3 km/1.8 miles) for sunset *(p108)*. Arrive by 5:30pm and watch thousands of herons and egrets roosting in the treetops. Return to Ubud for a traditional dance show at 7pm in the courtyard at the royal palace, Puri Saren *(p96)*, and then dine at a traditional *warung* in the town centre.

Day 2

Yoga lovers should take the opportunity to salute the sun with a yoga session *(www. theyogabarn.com)*. You'll need your own transport, or a car and driver, for the rest of the day for visiting Goa Gajah cave and temple *(p106)* before continuing on to lunch with a view at Kafe Kawi (inside the entrance of Pura Gunung Kawi) and an exploration of the temples at Tampaksiring (13 km/8 miles) *(p110)*. In the evening, check out Laughing Buddha Bar in central Ubud *(www.laughingbuddhabali.com)* for live music.

Day 3

Visit Neka Art Museum *(p98)* for a a superb introduction to Balinese art. Walk 500 m (546 yards) to Indus Restaurant *(www.casa lunabali.com/indus-restaurant)* for lunch with a view across the valley. Afterwards, head to Jungle Fish Pool Club *(www. chapung.com/ubud)*, in a stunning setting overhanging a river gorge, 4.5 km (3 miles) from Indus. Spend the afternoon relaxing by the pool. In the evening, chill out in the XL Shisha Lounge *(Jalan Monkey Forest 129)* with a shisha pipe and live music.

Day 4

Hire a car and tour-guide driver (we recommend *www.putu-bali.com*) and head to Kintamani to explore the lava fields at Mount Batur *(p120)*. Lunch on the rim of the caldera with spectacular volcano and lake views. Visit Pura Ulun Danu Batur temple *(p122)* and drive back to Ubud via Tegallalang *(p108)*, where there are stunning rice terraces. Stop for a drink at Kampung Cafe *(p109)*, and shop for handicrafts from a multitude of workshop outlets. Spend your evening at Betelnut *(Jalan Raya Ubud)*, where you can enjoy delicious Asian cuisine and perhaps a movie night, a talk, a dance performance or live music

Day 5

Visit Puri Lukisan art museum *(www. purilukisanmuseum.com)*, followed by some of the art shops and contemporary galleries in Ubud centre. Have lunch at the legendary Murni's Warung *(p98)*. In the afternoon, be eased into a state of total relaxation at Maya Ubud Spa *(p39)* – book in advance. Treat yourself to dinner at Hujan Locale *(www.hujanlocale.com)*, followed by cocktails and live music at No Mas Bar *(www.nomasubud.com)*.

→

1 Hindu ceremony at Ulun Danu Bratan temple.

2 Huge trees in the tropical jungle near Lake Tamblingan.

3 Balinese cocoa beans – some of the best in the world.

4 Munduk waterfall, a short walk from Munduk village.

3 DAYS
In Bali's Lake District

Day 1

Morning Begin at Mengwi at the Junglegold Bali organic chocolate factory *(www.jungle goldbali.com)* for a tour and a tasting of the delicious products. Then drive to Baturiti, visit the traditional produce market and make a photo-stop looking east towards Mount Batur and Mount Agung. The small lakeside market town of Bedugul *(p166)* is heralded by a corn and cabbage statue. Turn left here onto Jalan Kebun Raya and stop for lunch at Eat Drink Love Café & Art Shop.

Afternoon Wander through the cool, shaded Bali Botanic Garden, with over 2,000 species of plants *(p166)*. Then, for a change of pace, fly from tree to tree on rope nets and zip lines at the nearby Sila Agrotourism *(www.thesilasagrotourism.com)*.

Evening Head back to Bedugul to Warung Recreasi near Lake Bratan *(www.warung rekreasibedugul.com)*, a good option for both accommodation and dinner.

Day 2

Morning Golfers can enjoy an early-morning round at the spectacular Handara Golf Course *(www.handaragolfresort.com)*, the only golf course in the world that sits inside the crater of an extinct volcano. Others may enjoy browsing Bukit Mungsu market *(opposite Warung Recreasi)*, which has handicrafts and souvenirs, plus fruit and spices. Be sure to visit the mystical Ulun Danu Bratan Temple *(p166)* and have a taste of the locally grown strawberries at Strawberry Stop *(Jalan Raya)* beside the lake. Continue northwest along the main road. At the top of the hill, turn left towards Munduk village *(p165)*. This scenic route follows the rim of the ancient caldera and overlooks the northern shores of the twin lakes of Buyan and Tamblingan. Stop at Wanagiri Hidden Hills & Bali Swing, where viewing points invite you to pose for enviable Instagram photos. Continue to Munduk to The View Restaurant *(Jalan Raya Kayu Putih; www.plataran.com/the-view-munduk)* for glorious views of the valley and a lunch of Indonesian delights.

Afternoon Enjoy a gentle trek through clove and coffee plantations to splash at three of the famous waterfalls: Munduk, Melanting and Laangan Melanting. The round trip takes about two hours.

Evening Stay overnight at Munduk, where accommodation is plentiful.

Day 3

Morning Head to the southwest side of Lake Tamblingan *(p165)*, where local guides will row you across the tranquil waters in a traditional canoe. Visit Pura Tahun and other hidden temples and trek through the tropical forest. Lunch at Ngiring Ngewedang *(www.ngiring ngewedang.com)* and relish the jaw-dropping vista.

Afternoon Walk 2.5 km (1.6 miles) to the tiny village of Munduk Tamblingan to see the Pura Dalem Gubug lakeside temple, with its tall *meru* on a small promontory. The sight is marvellous, but there are more hidden temples to explore. The best way to reach them is by taking a guided canoe tour across the lake. Once you are back on dry land, follow the path that leads through open pasture back to the village of Gubug. Spend the rest of the day relaxing at your leisure.

Bali's Rice Fields

Bali is renowned for the beauty of its sculpted rice terraces. Estimated to cover 20 per cent of Bali's land mass, these vibrant-green, layered plantings unfold like giant stairways descending from the mountains to the sea. The magnificence of these gorgeous hand-carved landscapes can fill entire memory cards with remarkable photographs.

Lush, terraced rice fields, with Mount Agung in the background

BALI AND LOMBOK FOR
NATURAL WONDERS

It goes without saying that the islands of Bali and Lombok have natural beauty in abundance. Volcanoes soar into the clouds, waterfalls cascade down forested valleys, and primeval calderas etch and gouge the landscape – all this and an inevitably stunning coastline, too.

Volcanic Peaks

Hiking up Lombok's Mount Rinjani is one of the most exhilarating experiences in Indonesia. A four-hour trek ascending 850 m (2,800 ft) above the village of Sembalun will reward you with a magnificent view of Propok – a dramatic flat valley and fertile green plain surrounded by mountains and tropical forest.

↑ The small, active volcano and lake inside the caldera of Mount Rinjani

Dizzying Cliffs and Coral Reefs

Soaring limestone sea cliffs typify Bali's Bukit Peninsula and the island of Nusa Penida. Seaweed farms layer the shallows like patchwork quilts, and ribbons of luminous turquoise water highlight coral reefs and an aquatic world reminiscent of a living kaleidoscope. Here, the powerful swells of the Indian Ocean create some of the world's most thrilling and sought-after surf breaks. There is a beautiful variety of coral in the waters around the Gili Islands off Lombok, which teem with pipe fish, lionfish, moray eels, turtles and much more.

← Cliff in the shape of a Tyrannosaurus Rex at Kelingking Beach, Nusa Penida, and *(inset)* a sea turtle

Did You Know?

Bird-watchers can see well over 200 of Indonesia's bird species in Bali and Lombok.

Waterfalls

Sometimes the most spectacular natural wonders are the ones that are hardest to reach. Getting to Sekumpul Waterfall in Buleleng Regency in North Bali involves a three-hour hike past durian, rambutan and coffee plantations, complete with dirt tracks, crossings over streams and climbing about one hundred steps. The beautiful 80-m- (262-ft-) high waterfall is actually a cluster of six to seven narrow cascades that form the centrepiece of a lush-green bamboo-forested valley. These cascades are fed by two upland streams, and are the most accessible of a collection of falls within the area.

↑ The stunning Sekumpul Waterfall in North Bali, surrounded by greenery

◁ Balinese Cuisine

Considered to be one of the world's most complex cuisines, Balinese food is a blend of fresh ingredients, intricate flavours and aromatic spices. Shaped by Indigenous traditions, and Chinese and Indian influences, it is very different to typical Indonesian cuisine.

Indonesian Spices ▷

Indonesian cuisine is distinguished by the many freshly ground and blended spices that enliven and add depth to the dishes. Typical spices include ginger, turmeric, galangal, coriander, lemongrass and chillies, enhanced with shallots, garlic, candlenuts, pandan leaves and tamarind. The proper combination is regarded as an art in Indonesia, and delicate adjustments are made until the exact balance of flavours is achieved.

BALI AND LOMBOK FOR
FOOD LOVERS

The endless dining possibilities in Bali, and to a lesser extent in Lombok, cater to every taste, from *kaki-lima* (street-food carts) and tiny street-side stalls known as *warung* or *rumah makan* ("eating house") to seafood restaurants, vegan cafés and gourmet fine dining.

◁ Delicious Mangosteen

With a flavour said to be reminiscent of a fine peach, muscatel grapes and something indescribable which no other fruit has, it's not surprising that the mangosteen is held to be the most delectable of all Indonesia's tropical fruits. It is comprised of a deep-purple shell housing several segments of soft, juicy, pure-white pulp. The number of segments inside matches the number of petals found on the bottom of the shell.

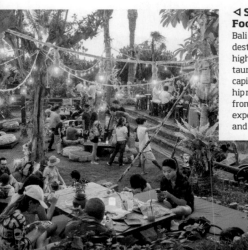

◁ Seminyak, Bali's Foodie Capital

Bali has emerged as a major culinary destination in the 21st century. With the highest concentration of independent restaurants on the island, Seminyak is its foodie capital. An abundance of uber-cool cafés and hip restaurants serve sensational cuisine from all around the world. The fine-dining experiences are enhanced by designer decor and celebrity chefs. Bon appétit!

Did You Know?

Food colourings are obtained from plants such as red hibiscus flowers and green pandan leaves.

◁ Jajan Pasar

Traditional Indonesian snacks and cakes, *jajan pasar* are steamed rather than baked, and therefore very different in texture, taste and appearance from Western cakes or pastries. Many of these moist, colourful delicacies are made with rice flour, coconut milk and palm sugar. Other ingredients might include cassava, tapioca, sago flour, eggs or mashed sweet potato. Typical flavourings are vanilla, durian and chocolate, while fillings often comprise beans, cheese and banana, or meat and carrots.

GET COOKING

The best way to find out more about the local cuisine is to sign up for a stimulating, hands-on cooking class in which you will learn how to prepare the basic *bumbu* spice mix, before going on to cook a complete feast that you can later savour at leisure. Classes are available in Bali and Lombok, and typically run for a full morning, followed by the chance to sample the fruits of your labour at lunchtime. Recommended cooking schools are Bumbu Bali in Tanjung Benoa and Gili Cooking Classes on Gili Air.

△ Fiery Lombok

For a destination with a name that loosely translates as "chilli", it's not surprising that Lombok's cuisine is highly regarded. You'll find a profusion of tastes, textures and aromas, with more than a few spicy surprises. If you prefer fine dining to street eats, you can savour classic Sasak flavours alongside familiar global fare, from Italian to Indian, in the main areas of Kuta, Senggigi and the Gili Islands.

Treetop Adventures

Hop from tree to tree at the fun Sila's Agrotourism *(www. thesilasagrotourism.com)*, an outdoor recreation park near Bedugul. Suspended bridges, winches, ropes, nets and flying-fox ziplines let visitors explore the forest from well above the ground. Not a fan of heights? This 10-ha (25-acre) park also has a Ferris wheel, and quad-bike and cycling adventures.

$\rightarrow$

The colourful Ferris wheel at Sila's Agrotourism

BALI AND LOMBOK FOR
FAMILIES

Surrounded as they are by water, it's no surprise that Bali and Lombok offer plentiful activities for adventurous families. Take to the water with a snorkel or for a swim, or perhaps add a dose of adrenaline at a water-based theme park.

Snorkelling and Swimming

Many of Lombok's pristine white-sand beaches are perfect for swimming and snorkelling, with clear turquoise water. Mawun Beach *(p187)* and the eastern side of Tanjung Aan Beach *(p186)* have sheltered bays. After swimming at Senggigi Beach be sure to watch the spectacular crimson sunset against a dramatic backdrop of the mighty Gunung Agung.

Snorkelling among corals in the clear waters off Lombok $\uparrow$

Turtle Release

The green and hawksbill turtles that inhabit Indonesia's coastal waters are considered endangered due to harvesting for meat, eggs and shells. Additionally, their existence is threatened by the loss of nesting grounds and water pollution. Turtle conservation initiatives in Bali retrieve the eggs and ensure they are incubated in a secured environment. The hatchlings are then cared for in a holding tank until they are strong enough to swim in the ocean. The heart-warming experience of releasing baby turtles, organized by the Bali Sea Turtle Society *(www.baliseaturtle.org)* in Kuta between April and October, is especially popular with children, teaching them about conservation from an early age.

←

Baby sea turtles being released, and *(inset)* Hawksbill turtle hatchlings in a holding tank

> **INSIDER TIP**
> **Surf's Up**
>
> After watching the pros hit the waves, your little ones might want to try surfing themselves. Many accredited surf schools on the island, such as Up2U in Kuta, run sessions just for kids *(www.up2usurf school.com)*.

Get Wet at Waterbom

Voted the best of its kind in Asia, Waterbom Bali *(www.waterbom-bali.com)* is a fabulous theme park for a family day out, with rides, slides and leisure attractions to suit kids and adults of all ages. Waterslides include the Constrictor – a staggering 250 m (820 ft) in length – the Python, the Boomerang, the Pipeline and Climax, where you can reach speeds of up to 43 mph (70 kmph).

→

Floating down a stream at the fun Waterbom Bali

The Bali Spa Experience

For a true escape, stay at one of Bali's exclusive spa retreats. Utilizing natural products and local village remedies is the universal concept of these establishments. In addition to traditional Balinese massage, treatments may include Ayurvedics, hot stone massage, Thai massage and barefoot Shiatsu. Energy treatment may include Watsu, in which the participant floats effortlessly while receiving gentle, water-assisted massage and stretches; chakra balancing sessions; craniosacral therapy; Reiki; and Chi Nei Tsang massage. Activities may include yoga, martial arts and meditation.

→ Chakra balancing in an infinity pool at a spa retreat

BALI AND LOMBOK FOR
WELLNESS

Ease fatigue, stimulate the senses and awaken the spirit at one of the many spas in Bali and Lombok. As well as luxury spa retreats, most hotels and beauty salons offer traditional and modern body-soothing treatments to enhance your overall wellbeing.

Healing Boreh

Boreh is a centuries-old remedy, traditionally used by Balinese villagers to relieve muscular aches and pains and boost circulation after long days of toiling in the rice fields. Warm, potent spices such as powdered sandalwood, cloves, cinnamon, coriander, turmeric and nutmeg are blended with rice powder into a fragrant paste and applied to the body as a warming, healing masque. Balinese Boreh is one of the most luxurious spa treatments available – wonderful not only for its relaxing and curative properties but also for exfoliating and softening the skin.

→ Traditional Indonesian spices used in Balinese spa treatments

TOP 3 SPA RETREATS

Spa Alila, Manggis
🅦 alilahotels.com/
manggis/spa-alila
In a forest and
overlooking the
sea, this spa has two
bales for relaxing
treatments.

Maya Ubud Spa
🅦 spaatmaya.com/
ubud
This large retreat has
luxury rooms and villas
and captures the spirit
of a Balinese village.

Prana Spa, Seminyak
📞 811 3861 761
Indulge in the beauty
rituals of ancient kings
and queens at this spa.

A Balinese open-
sided thatch *bale* for
massage treatments ↑

MANDI LULUR

Indonesia's famous
Mandi Lulur skin
care treatment ori-
ginated in the royal
palaces of Central
Java. The ritual begins
with a body massage,
followed by a skin
exfoliation utilizing a
fragrant paste blended
from sandalwood,
turmeric, ground nuts,
rice, herbs, jasmine
flowers and other
ingredients. The relax-
ing indulgence is then
completed with a
yogurt body mask.

↑ A relaxing head massage,
improving blood flow for
healthier skin

Massage

If it's massage you're after, check out Jari Menari (the name
means "Dancing Fingers"), which has branches in Seminyak
and Nusa Dua. Winner of multiple awards, it has highly trained,
all-male practitioners who focus on rhythm, flow and long
connective strokes, with strong, firm, consistent pressure.
The semi-open-air massage rooms are elegant and full of
natural light, each bordering a koi fish pond. If you're interested
in learning how to administer a massage, you can join one of
Jari Menari's regular day-long Learn Massage Workshops
(*www.jarimenari.com*).

Bali's Virgin Beach

Located near Candi Dasa, Virgin Beach, or Pasir Putih, meaning "white sands", is fringed by a coconut grove and flanked by green headlands *(p139)*. This idyllic stretch of sand is easily accessed by car, but a more romantic approach is by sea in a traditional *jukung* fishing boat. Contact Paleng's Bali for details *(www. palengsbali.com)*.

Virgin Beach, where you can rent sun loungers and umbrellas

BALI AND LOMBOK FOR
BEACH LOVERS

Want to spend some time on the beach? You've come to the right place. Lounge on a sandy stretch with your holiday read, rent a surfboard and take to the waves, or simply relax and enjoy the view. And what a view: Bali's coastline has an ever-shifting palette of colours, just waiting to be enjoyed.

PICTURE PERFECT
Kelingking Beach

Indonesian for "little finger", Kelingking is Nusa Penida's most Instagrammed beach – a secluded golden-sand haven surrounded by turquoise waters at the bottom of a lofty cliff *(p33)*. Getting to the beach involves a hike down a 400-m (1,310-ft) perilously steep, narrow cliff-side track, so most people are content to photograph it from the cliff top.

Lombok's Southern Shores

Some of Lombok's most spectacular coastal scenery can be found on the southern shores of the island around Kuta, which presents a very different picture from its celebrated namesake in Bali. Here, windswept white- and golden-sand bays are separated by headlands and rocky outcrops. The glorious crescent-shaped beaches of Kuta and Tanjung Aan are famous for their surf breaks but when the tide is out, the bays turn into shallow pools of turquoise water *(p186)*.

The tropical paradise of Kuta Beach, Lombok, with clear turquoise water

Dream Beach, with its ↑ white sand and blue sea, Nusa Lembongan

Dream Beach, Nusa Lembongan

On the island of Nusa Lembongan *(p89)* off the south coast of Bali, Dream Beach is a gorgeous, secluded half-moon of powdery white sand backed by mangroves. A restaurant, beach club and hut-style accommodation can be found on the cliff above this pandanus-fringed bay. Be sure to visit the nearby Devil's Tear – a rocky outcrop and cove, where you'll see dramatic waves crashing at full power to create water plumes and high-pressure spouts; just don't be tempted to get too close to the edge.

> **HIDDEN GEM**
> **Pink Beach**
>
> The spectacular Pantai Tangsi, or Pink Beach, in Southeast Lombok is an offbeat side trip from Kuta. The beach's colour comes from fragments of red coral washed up on the shore, which, when mixed with the sand, give it a pink hue.

Bukit Peninsula

Bali's Bukit Peninsula *(pp82–6)* is home to some of the island's most idyllic beaches. Many of these beauty spots are at the base of towering cliffs and involve walking down steep steps to reach them. Hang around surfers in Bali and you will hear mention of Uluwatu, Padang Padang, Impossibles, Bingin, Dreamland, Balangan, Nyang Nyang and Green Bowl – world-class surf beaches named after waves that break on shallow reefs creating long tubes.

↑ Beach at Uluwatu, a world-famous surfing spot on the Bukit Peninsula, and *(inset)* surfer at Padang Padang

▽ Art Markets

Bali is well known for its busy art markets. Most present a rambling scene of small kiosks within a semi-open-air complex. Others, such as the huge Kumbasari Art Market in Denpasar (p70), are housed in a dedicated building. Crowded alleyways are crammed with vendors, buyers, artworks and handicrafts stretching in all directions. Haggling is essential and highly entertaining, with a lot of flamboyant gestures.

BALI AND LOMBOK FOR
ARTS AND CRAFTS

The arts of Bali and Lombok are inseparable from the cultural and religious life of the communities; whether performing arts, painting or handicrafts, art in every form is the pinnacle of local culture. Individual villages in Bali and Lombok support specific crafts and art forms.

△ The Art of Batik

An ancient Indonesian art form, Batik designs are created by covering part of a fabric with wax and then dyeing it. The dye doesn't penetrate the wax, which is then melted away, before being reapplied to leave behind intricate multicoloured patterns. Motifs drawn with a wax-filled pen are called batik tulis. The wax can also be applied with a copper stamp, known as a cap.

INTERNATIONAL DEMAND

The rich artistic traditions of Bali have led to the evolution of a vibrant handicraft industry, in which pieces are created to be sold in local art shops and markets, as well as for export worldwide, providing business opportunities for many locals. Souvenirs and art objects range from trinkets, clothing, kites, woodcarvings and paintings to rare collectors' items.

▽ Art of Stone

Every kind of stone sculpture is produced on Bali, and styles vary from village to village, with many intricate designs for places of worship. Interestingly, there is little difference between the iconography decorating temples and that of private homes. Gateways represent the dividing line between the inner and outer worlds and, as such, are the recipients of some of the most fantastic carvings. Bali's main centre of stone carving is the village of Batubulan (p102).

△ Woodcarving

In Bali's woodcarving villages such as Mas (p105) and Tegallalang (p108), you will hear the gentle hammering and sanding of the woodcarvers as they sit cross-legged, surrounded by piles of woodchips. Using small tools and highly sharpened instruments, the master carver lightly taps, chips, chisels and picks away to create effigies, masks and ornaments.

Pottery ▷

Pottery is the main product of several villages in Lombok. Water decanters, decorated plates and saucers, vases, huge water containers and lamps are all created by hand. The pots crafted in Banyumulek (p189) are simple in design and devoid of embellishments; Masbagik specializes in distinctive geometric patterns and Penujak (p185) produces pots decorated with animal motifs.

◁ Natural Materials

A wide range of handicrafts, both practical and decorative, are made from natural fibres and materials, such as pandanus, rattan, banana leaves, bamboo, roots and grasses, bone, coconut shell and buffalo horn. Natural ornamentation is used to embellish these objects. You will even find boxes and model ships made entirely from cloves.

Splash Out

Bali's Tanjung Benoa *(p82)* has operators offering everything from wakeboarding, jet-skiing, parasailing and kayaking to banana boat rides and flying fish – an inflatable rubber boat that is pulled by a speedboat and flies up in the air. For all of these adventure watersports in Lombok, head to Senggigi *(p180)* or the Gili Islands *(p174)*.

←

Tandem parasailing, one of the popular watersports at Tanjung Benoa, Bali

BALI AND LOMBOK FOR
ADVENTURERS

The seas off Bali and Lombok provide plenty of opportunity for surfing, sailing, diving and all manner of other watersports. Inland, you can climb volcanoes, raft rivers, go canyoning through deep river gorges or try your hand at paragliding off cliff tops.

Go Canyoning

Bali and Lombok's vast river systems flow through deep canyon gorges. Canyoning, led by ICO Pro qualified instructors, involves following a river downstream while negotiating boulders, waterfalls and natural slides by trekking, caving, scrambling, climbing, abseiling, jumping, sliding and swimming. Established canyoning routes are near Bedugul and Kintamani in Bali and near Gumantar Village in North Lombok. The easiest trip takes about 1.5 hours and the more advanced routes can take 3–4 hours to complete. Canyoning.id *(www.canyoning.id)* and Adventure & Spirit *(www. adventureandspirit.com)* organize expeditions for all levels.

→

Bali's stunning, rugged Beji Guwang Hidden Canyon, Sukawati

 PICTURE PERFECT
Jet of Energy

The magnificent jet of pure-white energy of the Tiu Kelep waterfall near Senaru in Lombok makes for a fantastic photo. You can swim in the pool below it *(p183)*.

Climb Mount Rinjani

If the idea of jumping out of your comfort zone and pushing yourself physically and mentally appeals, then you should challenge yourself to climb Lombok's eerily beautiful Mount Rinjani *(p172)*. The three-day and two-night trek to the summit is a true bucket-list experience where you can swim in the crater lake next to the active, smoking cone of Rinjani's Gunung Baru and sleep in a tent teetering on the side of a crater rim.

→

Camping site on the ascent to the summit of Mount Rinjani, Lombok

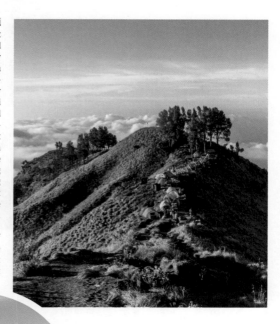

Soar Like an Eagle

The best place for paragliding is Bali's Timbis Beach. Book a tandem glide with Bali Paragliding *(www.baliparagliding.com)* and soar along the shores of the Indian Ocean beside picturesque cliffs. Every year, from May to October, the southerly trade winds blow in off the Indian Ocean and allow for a 12-km (7.5-mile) flight above the sea.

←

Paragliding above the Indian Ocean off Timbis Beach on the Bukit Peninsula, South Bali

Raft Rivers

Enjoy rafting on Bali's Ayung and Telaga Waja rivers against a backdrop of jungle, gorges, waterfalls and rice terraces. Wira Rafting Bali's professionally trained guides will give you instruction and work with you to safely navigate the raft through torrents, twists, tight turns and inclined rapids *(www. raftingbali.net)*. If you like it particularly wild, go during the rainy season (Oct–Apr).

→

Whitewater rafting through the Ayung River Gorge in Ubud, Bali, a thrilling adventure

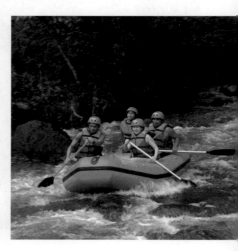

Canang Sari

Offerings to the gods are an integral part of day-to-day life for the Balinese, and can be seen everywhere in many different forms. When you walk down the street in Bali, you will most certainly notice the tiny, woven palm-frond trays that have been placed on the pavements and at the base of steps. These offerings, known as *canang sari*, are presented twice a day, with devotion, in front of homes and businesses, as well as at temples and shrines, on statues and even at crossroads, where they are believed to ward off accidents.

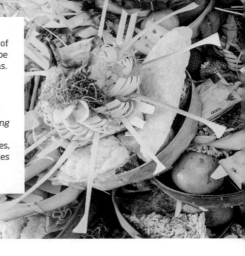

→

Palm-frond trays containing typical *canang sari* offerings

BALI AND LOMBOK FOR
LOCAL CULTURE

There are many places to immerse yourself in Bali and Lombok's unique cultures. Sample local delicacies at night markets, visit museums, watch shows of dance performances and ritual music, witness Balinese Hindu and Lombok Sasak religious ceremonies or visit traditional villages.

Sasak man playing a Gendang Beleq drum in a village in Lombok ↑

Gendang Beleq

The distinctive music of Lombok, Gendang Beleq forms an important part of the island's culture. At most major events and ceremonies you will see a band of colourfully dressed musicians, playing, dancing and marching with their drums and other instruments.

GREAT VIEW
Rice Terraces

Jatiluwih village *(p160),* with its spellbinding vista of rolling rice terraces, is a UNESCO World Heritage Site for its preservation of traditional Balinese farming techniques.

INSIDER TIP
Where to See Dance Shows

Dance performances geared for tourists last 90 minutes. These are not inferior to sacred performances; in fact, some of the islands' best dancers and musicians perform for tourists. Many large hotels have regular evening dinner shows. Various forms of dance and drama can be seen at the annual Bali Arts Festival too *(p52)*.

Dance Performances

The roots of Balinese dance are trance ritual and the Javanese theatrical forms known as *wayang,* where performers wear colourful masks and headdresses. Kecak dance is based on a trance formerly used in times of epidemic. Performances take place at religious ceremonies. In Lombok, the dances of the Sasak are ritual performances, often involving men in competition or combat.

←

A Balinese dancer in traditional make-up and costume

Rice Field Irrigation

Because of the island's long dry season, irrigation is critical to Balinese wet-rice agriculture. This is achieved through ancient aquatic engineering, managed by the farmers through village cooperatives known as *subak.* Water is diverted from rivers and streams and channelled through an elaborate system of canals, tunnels and aqueducts to the top of terraced rice fields. It then flows by gravity from field to field.

↑ Rice fields in Bali, watered by an irrigation system dating to the 11th century

47

The Lofty Stone Coconut Shell Temple

High on the slopes of Gunung Batukaru is Pura Luhur Batukaru *(p160)*, the "Lofty Stone Coconut Shell Temple", which venerates the deities of mountains and lakes, and was the ancestral temple for the royal family of Tabanan, whose descendants still maintain the shrines today. Make time to explore this mystical and deeply spiritual place, pausing for a while to contemplate or meditate.

→

Pavilions in Pura Luhur Batukaru, located on the slopes of Gunung Batukaru

BALI FOR
BEAUTIFUL TEMPLES

The temple or Pura is the focus of the spiritual activity of every community in Bali, a transient abode for the gods to occupy whenever they are invited. Open and unroofed for easy access between the worlds, the gates and walls serve only to keep impure and evil influences away.

Pura Kehen

A little off the main tourist path, but well worth a visit, is Pura Kehen *(p136)*, the state temple of the Bangli kingdom and the second largest in Bali. It is also one of the island's most beautiful and impressive temples, set on a wooded hillside in terraces lined with religious statues.

→

Pura Kehen temple, the former royal temple of the Bangli kingdom

 PICTURE PERFECT
Island Temple

Pura Tanah Lot *(p156)* is one of the most photographed sights in Bali. In the late afternoon, you can see a splendid profile of the temple silhouetted against the setting sun.

Pura Dalem Jagaraga

The lavishly decorated Pura Dalem Jagaraga near Singaraja (p167) is famous for its flamboyant stone carvings. The elaborate sculptured panels portray life during Dutch colonial times, including a Dutch steamer sending out a smoky SOS signal while being attacked by a sea monster, armed bandits holding up two smug Europeans riding in a vintage Ford car and World War II bi-planes engaged in an aerial battle, with some plunging into the sea.

← Detail of a stone carving on the Pura Dalem Jagaraga

Temple Processions

Any visitor who spends more than a few days in Bali is likely to see some kind of fascinating temple festival or colourful procession, an important and integral element of daily life on the island. In these processions, women carry stunningly crafted *gebogan* – mountain-shaped offerings of fruit on their heads. A lavish festival that commemorates the founding of a temple is called an Odalan.

↑ Devotees carrying elaborate, colourful offerings in a temple procession in Ubud

Gunung Batukaru

The extinct volcano of Batukaru (or Batukau) in Bali's Tabanan Regency is the island's second-highest peak (*p160*). Located in an area with the greatest biological diversity in Bali, its high alpine slopes are filled with mountain streams, ferns, wild flowers, creepers and orchids, as well as the rare black leaf-eating monkey, small forest deer, butterflies, flying lizards, the *landak* (porcupine) and the *lubak* (mongoose). Local guides lead visitors on anything from gentle hikes to challenging treks to the 2,276-m (7,500-ft) summit.

→

Gunung Batukaru, the source of irrigation water for the surrounding rice, coffee and fruit fields

BALI AND LOMBOK FOR
SPECTACULAR VOLCANOES

Bali and Lombok sit on the volcanic "ring of fire" that stretches from Sumatra to the Banda Sea. The resplendent summits of Gunung Agung and Gunung Rinjani dominate the landscapes of these two neighbouring islands.

Gunung Seraya

At an elevation of 1,090 m (3,500 ft), Gunung Seraya towers over Bali's most easterly coast. For a gentle hike, start at Bangle village on the eastern slope, in the company of a guide, and trek to Toye Masem – the Five Holy Springs. The source of each spring is guarded by a shrine and is purported to spout a different taste. The ambitious can aim for the summit, which challenges even the most experienced hikers – at the top you will be rewarded with a breathtaking vista.

←

Gunung Seraya and Gunung Lempuyang seen against a backdrop of rice terraces

🔘 PICTURE PERFECT
Volcano and Rice Fields

On a clear day at sunrise, the central and eastern volcanoes of the mighty Gunung Batukaru make a dramatic appearance across the fields to create a backdrop to a perfect photo.

← Trekking Gunung Batukaru at sunrise, worth the challenge for the views at its summit

Gunung Catur

Standing on the eastern side of Lake Bratan *(p166)* is the extinct Gunung Catur. At 1,861 m (6,100 ft), it is the fourth-highest mountain in Bali, with dense forest covering its slopes. The hike to the top takes about three hours amid gorgeous scenery. You will see long-tailed monkeys and pass various shrines and former Dutch colonial weekend retreats. The view from the summit, looking down over Lake Tamblingan, is spectacular. On the rim of the caldera is the Pura Pucak Mangu temple, built around 1830.

🔍 HIDDEN GEM
Crater Lake

The caldera of Lombok's Gunung Rinjani *(p172)* is partially filled by a dazzling, mystifyingly blue, crescent-shaped crater lake, with waterfalls, natural hot springs, and the volcanic cone of Gunung Baru ("new mountain") budding in its centre. This hidden gem on the mountain's summit is visible only to hardy climbers.

↑ Lake Tamblingan, seen from the edge of the caldera of Gunung Catur

A YEAR IN
BALI AND LOMBOK

JANUARY

△ **Chinese New Year** *(Jan/Feb)*. Observed by Balinese and Sasaks of Chinese descent, Chinese New Year is celebrated with festive dinners, decorations and Chinese *barongsai* lion and dragon dance troupes.

FEBRUARY

△ **Galungan** *(varies)*. Taking place every 210 days according to the Balinese calendar, this holiday marks the descent of ancestral spirits and Balinese deities to earth.

Bau Nyale Festival *(Feb/Mar)*. Lombok's most popular festival takes place on the beaches around Kuta when thousands of colourful sea worms are washed ashore. The worms are eaten and there is traditional dance and music.

MAY

△ **Takbir Parade** *(May/Jun 2019 – varies)*. The people of Lombok hold a parade to celebrate the end of Ramadan. It is unique to the island.

JUNE

△ **Bali Arts Festival** *(mid-Jun–mid-Jul)*. A month-long festival of Balinese artistic traditions and culture takes place in Denpasar. There are shows of traditional and contemporary dance, shadow puppetry, concerts and art exhibitions.

SEPTEMBER

△ **Senggigi Festival** *(early Sep)*. A four-day celebration of Lombok's art and culture, with street theatre, traditional music and dance, and handicrafts and street-food stalls.

Balinale International Film Festival *(late Sep)*. This week-long festival has a packed programme of award-winning films and movie premieres showcasing Indonesia's best talent.

OCTOBER

△ **Ubud Writers and Readers Festival** *(early Oct)*. Attracting literature enthusiasts from all over the world, this festival provides intellectual and sensory stimulation via interviews, readings, poetry slams and book launches.

Nusa Dua Fiesta *(mid-Oct)*. A week of art exhibitions, theatre performances, fashion shows and food bazaars.

MARCH

△ **Pengrupukan** (early or mid-Mar). Lively processions are held all over Bali to drive away the evil spirits with gongs, drums, cymbals and ogoh-ogoh papier-mâché monsters on the eve of Nyepi.

Nyepi (mid-/late Mar). The Hindu "day of silence" is a public holiday with fasting and meditation. The airport and all businesses are closed, there is no one out on the streets and all lights are extinguished.

APRIL

△ **Bali Spirit Festival** (early Apr). This energy-filled festival in Ubud showcases leading practitioners in health, yoga, wellbeing, world music, community programmes and environmental conservation.

Ubud Food Festival (mid-Apr). A three-day event to tantalize the taste buds with a huge variety of Balinese and international dishes.

Gendang Beleq Festival (mid-Apr). Big-drum musical troupes gather all over Lombok to accompany colourful dances.

JULY

△ **Stick Fighting Festival** (Jul). Senggigi is the best place to see this Lombok event where men compete with wooden sticks and shields to show off their strength and agility to the accompaniment of traditional music.

Bali Kite Festival (Jul/Aug). Traditional giant kites, up to 4 x 10 m (13 x 33 ft) in size, are made and flown in competitions by teams from different villages.

AUGUST

△ **Independence Day** (17 Aug). This national holiday marks Indonesia's freedom from colonialism. People decorate their houses in red and white and display the national flag. Children participate in fun games.

Ubud Village Jazz Festival (mid-Aug). Jazz legends and rising stars from Indonesia and all over the world perform at this two-day festival.

DECEMBER

△ **Mulang Pekelem** (Dec). Hindus in Lombok make a full-moon pilgrimage to Lake Segara Arak in Mount Rinjani's crater.

Perang Topat (Dec). Taking place at the Pura Lingsar temple in Lombok, Hindus and Muslims pray for another year of good crops before engaging in a frivolous rice-snack food fight.

NOVEMBER

△ **Badung Art and Cultural Festival** (mid-Nov). A week-long bonanza of Balinese art, dance and other cultural traditions.

A BRIEF
HISTORY

Two tiny islands in the archipelago that makes up Indonesia, Bali and Lombok's strategic position and natural beauty have caught the attention of neighbouring East Java, Dutch colonizers and the global tourism industry. Each has played its part in shaping the islands' history and characters.

Early Human History

While it's known that Homo Sapiens reached present-day Indonesia between 60,000 and 45,000 years ago, Bali and Lombok's early recorded history is scant. Evidence suggests that Stone Age people were the first to land on Bali, where they lived in temporary caves and made tools from animal bones. Later, in around 1,500 BC, these people were joined by seafaring Austronesian ethnic groups, who were migrating from China into Southeast Asia and the Pacific. By the 3rd century AD, Bronze Age people of Chinese and Vietnamese descent arrived, settling in Gilimanuk and farming the surrounding land.

1. An 18th-century Dutch map of Bali and Lombok.

2. Pura Maospahit statue, Denpasar, capital of the Majapahit kingdom.

3. Dutch engraving of a Balinese king and his entourage, 1597.

4. A photograph taken in Lombok at the time of the Dutch invasion in 1894.

Timeline of events

2,500 BC

Evidence suggests Stone Age people lived on Bali.

AD 414

Chinese records mention two schools of Hinduism in Java on the Indonesian mainland.

1293

Majapahit kingdom established.

1343

Majapahit invasion of Bali by Javanese ruler and general Gajah Mada, who defeated the king in Bedulu.

The Balinese Kingdoms

For centuries, Bali and Lombok escaped the encroachment of Java, the largest of present-day Indonesia's islands, just off Bali's western shore. In 1478, this changed when the Hindu Majapahit kings fled to Bali from East Java after being defeated by the Muslim Demak Sultanate, who hailed from Java's north coast. The Majapahit's rule of Bali was short-lived. By 1550, the island was subsumed by King Dalam Baturenggong of the kingdom of Gelgel, who created a single kingdom stretching from East Java to the island of Sumbawa.

Lombok, meanwhile, maintained its independence from both Java and Bali until the 17th century, when Makassar groups invaded eastern Lombok from their colonies in neighbouring Sumbawa and the Karangasem people crossed the Lombok Strait from the east of Bali and settled in western Lombok. A period of infighting between the competing feudal kingdoms on both Bali and Lombok followed. As a result, the Gelgel kingdom broke down in 1651 and Bali was divided into nine separate kingdoms. Later, in 1750, Lombok was split into four kingdoms: Pagesangan, Pagutan, Mataram and Cakranegara.

↑ Statue of Gajah Mada, ruler of the Hindu empire of Majapahit

Early 1500s

Hindu-Javanese priests and artisans emigrate to Bali seeking exile from Islamic empires dominating Java.

1597

The first Dutch trading ships arrive in Bali searching for spices. The Western world receives fascinating reports about the island.

1651

Bali is split into nine kingdoms: Klungkung, Buleleng, Karangasem, Mengwi, Badung, Tabanan, Gianyar, Bangli and Jembrana.

1838

Lombok's four kingdoms unite and become part of the Mataram kingdom.

Dutch Rule

The Dutch merchant fleet had been a powerful force in Europe for centuries, but in the early 17th century it extended its horizons, developing a network of trade routes that stretched around the globe. The Dutch East India Company, founded in 1602, set its sights on Asia, exploiting its natural resources. In Bali, the company took advantage of the splintering kingdoms and seized control of large parts of the island: by 1849 northern and eastern Bali were under their control. Further expansion by the Dutch was met with fierce resistance – in 1906 the royal household of Badung presented themselves to Dutch officers and committed *puputan* (mass suicide); in 1908, the Klungkung household followed suit. In Lombok, meanwhile, the Dutch were seen to have liberated the island from Balinese control. In fact, colonialism caused a famine that tormented the island for nearly 50 years.

The Tourism Boom

Dutch reports of Bali and Lombok's beauty were hard to resist, prompting Europeans to make the arduous journey to the islands by boat. By 1930, Bali saw up to 100 visitors a month – a

THE LAST PARADISE

Early images of Bali by Dutch illustrator W O J Nieuwendamp and German photographer Gregor Krause inspired Westerners to visit the island. Some visitors stayed on more permanently, settling mainly in Ubud and Sanur, and presented to the outside world an image of Bali as "the island of the gods" where "everyone is an artist".

Timeline of events

1928
Opening of the first international hotel, the Bali Hotel, in Denpasar.

1942
Japanese invasion; Dutch withdraw from the archipelago.

1894
Dutch take over the whole of Lombok; Mataram is dismantled.

1908
Mass suicide by royal family in Klungkung; Dutch control all of Bali.

3

staggering amount by the standards of the time. In response to the island's growing number of visitors, the Dutch invested in infrastructure, starting a ferry service between Banyuwangi in East Java and Gilimanuk on Bali, building the island's first road and opening an airport in 1938. Bali and Lombok could now be reached from almost anywhere in the world.

The World Stage

Bali's newfound accessibility had a consequence – it was dragged into World War II when Japanese forces landed at Sanur and took over from the demoralized Dutch garrison. The fleet then sailed on to Lombok, where they soon defeated the Dutch and occupied the island. The Japanese ruled Bali and Lombok in accordance with the already established Dutch system, requisitioning food and causing famine and epidemics. At the end of the war, Indonesia seized the chance for independence, declaring nationalist leader Sukarno its first president. The Dutch, however, wanted their colony back; they retook Lombok and tried to reassert control in Bali, where they were fiercely resisted. The Dutch finally recognized Indonesia's independence in 1949.

① Poster for the Bali Hotel by Willem Gerard Hofke, 1920s. ↑

② The Dutch Reoccupation, 1946.

③ Declaration of Independence by President Sukarno, 1945.

Did You Know?

The last *puputan* in Balinese history happened on Gusti Ngurah Rai's command at Marga in 1946.

1946

The Dutch return; Colonel Gusti Ngurah Rai and 95 guerrilla fighters massacred by the Dutch.

1950

Bali and Lombok become part of Indonesia.

1945

Japan surrenders; Sukarno becomes president of Indonesia.

1956

Sukarno dismantles parliamentary democracy and ends free enterprise.

Sukarno and Suharto

Sukarno's presidency was fragile. The Indonesian economy had seriously deteriorated as a result of World War II and support for the Communist Party grew as a result. When Balinese volcano Gunung Agung erupted, it added further anguish. Over 1,600 people were killed and 100,000 displaced, while massive areas of arable land and crops were ruined, causing food shortages. The desperate population turned to the Communist Party, who staged an abortive coup d'état in Jakarta. In response, Sukarno delegated extensive powers to the chief of staff of the army, Suharto, who set out to extinguish all traces of Communism by killing Communist sympathizers, ethnic Chinese and other minorities. At least one million people died across Indonesia and the population grew fearful of Suharto and his forces.

The Second Tourism Boom

Suharto became president in 1967 and, with the support of the army and his "New Order" regime, ruled Indonesia with an iron fist. He effectively banned Islam, the dominant religion in Lombok. To fund his government, Suharto opened Indonesia

① Smoke emanating from Gunung Agung volcano on Bali in 1963.

② Tourists lounging under colourful umbrellas and on beanbags on Kuta Beach, Bali.

③ An aerial image of Bali's Nusa Dua Beach, one of the island's many resorts.

Timeline of events

1963

Gunung Agung erupts catastrophically, killing 1,600 and leaving 100,000 homeless.

1965–66

Controversial attempted coup; anti-Communist massacres follow - at least 500,000 are killed in Bali and Lombok.

1967

Suharto replaces Sukarno as president of Indonesia.

1971

Mass tourism programme launched by Indonesian government.

up to mass tourism and Bali became his paradigm. By the 1990s, the island welcomed 400,000 visitors a year and had become one of Indonesia's most prosperous provinces. Lombok, meanwhile, saw few visitors and lost out on the economic boom – a situation that was exacerbated in 2000 when militant Islamists attacked Chinese-, Christian- and Balinese-owned buildings on the island. Bali also saw terrorist attacks in 2002 and 2005, temporarily causing a downturn in the island's tourism industry.

Bali and Lombok Today

In 2019, President Joko Widodo announced the "10 New Balis" plan, which aimed to funnel tourism away from Bali and into Indonesia's other 18,307 islands. This initiative brought new investment to Lombok, including the Mandalika Resort Area, but attracted criticism by some who claimed that the deals were corrupt and lead to forced evictions. In 2020, the plan was stalled by the COVID-19 pandemic, which shattered Bali and Lombok's tourist-centric economies. Climate change also hit Indonesia hard, with the country experiencing 2,291 floods, landslides and hurricanes in 2020 alone.

↑ Red roses in the sand at the bomb blast scene in Jimbaran Bay, Bali , 2005

2000
Unrest in Lombok; hundreds of Chinese, Christian and Balinese homes, churches and businesses are looted and burned.

2018
Earthquakes strike Lombok, killing over 550.

1998
Economic crisis causes riots in Jakarta; President Suharto resigns.

2017
Gunung Agung becomes active; villagers evacuated.

2020–22
The COVID-19 pandemic hits Bali hard due to its reliance on tourism.

EXPERIENCE

SOUTH BALI AND THE BUKIT PENINSULA

At the heart of South Bali is Denpasar, the island's provincial capital since 1958 and today a busy city. From the late 18th to the early 20th century, Denpasar was the royal capital of the kingdom of Badung, which dominated the southern part of Bali at the time. Under King Kesiman, who ruled Badung from 1829 to 1863, the Dutch were allowed to establish a trading station in Kuta in 1826. When these Europeans tried to advance further into the province, they were met with fierce resistace, notably in 1906, when a parade of 4,000 Balinese men, women and children intercepted the Dutch at Badung's palace and committed *puputan* (mass ritual suicide).

In the 1930s, South Bali became the gateway to the island as a whole when the port was developed at Sanur and the airport built at Kuta. Resorts soon sprang up and by the 1960s South Bali was the island's tourism hot spot. The Bukit Peninsula, which is attached to the very south of Bali by a thin stetch of land, is a particularly popular place to stay thanks to its string of beaches.

Tangguntiti

Pande
Lumintang   Bindu
Sumerta

DENPASAR
❷
Sebudi

Kesiman Petilan

Sanur Kaja

Dauh Puri Klod
Panjer   Renon
Tegalwangi   Singgi
Penyaringan

B A D U N G   Batujimbar

Pegok   Sanur Kauh
Sidakarya
Sesetan   Belanjong   ❸ SANUR
Batan Kendal
Pesanggaran

Nusa Penida

B a d u n g
S t r a i t

❽
PULAU
SERANGAN

❿ TANJUNG
BENOA

Tengkulung

NUSA DUA
Bualu   ⓲
Peminge

Kesiman
Kertalangu

SOUTH BALI
AND THE BUKIT
PENINSULA

SOUTH BALI AND THE BUKIT PENINSULA

Must Sees
❶ Pura Luhur Uluwatu
❷ Denpasar
❸ Sanur
❹ Kuta and Legian

Experience More
❺ South Kuta Beach
❻ Seminyak
❼ Canggu
❽ Pulau Serangan
❾ Benoa Harbour
❿ Tanjung Benoa
⓫ Jimbaran
⓬ Garuda Wisnu Kencana
   Cultural Park
⓭ Padang Padang Beach
⓮ Pecatu
⓯ Bingin Beach
⓰ Uluwatu
⓱ Ungasan
⓲ Nusa Dua
⓳ Nusa Penida
⓴ Nusa Lembongan
㉑ Nusa Ceningan

Nusa Penida   Mambal   Gianyar   Padangbai

Sempidi   Sukawati   Goa Lawah

Badung Strait

Denpasar   Tohpati   NUSA
Canggu   LEMBONGAN
Legian   Sanur   ⓴
Kuta   Ped   Sampalan
         Toyapakeh
Benoa   ㉑   ⓳ NUSA
Harbour   NUSA   PENIDA
Jimbaran   CENINGAN
Nusa Dua   Sebuluh   Tanglad
Uluwatu
Pecatu   *Area of main map*

0 kilometres   15
0 miles   15

N

The three-tiered *meru*,
dedicated to Nirartha,
who achieved enlightenment
while meditating here →

1

PURA LUHUR ULUWATU

🗺 D5 ⌂ End of Jalan Uluwatu, Uluwatu 🚌 ⏰ 9am-6pm daily

Not only one of Bali's most sacred places of worship but also one of the most beautiful examples of Balinese architecture, Pura Luhur Uluwatu, on Bali's extreme southwesterly tip, is one of a series of sea temples dedicated to the guardian spirits of the ocean.

The temple's history is shrouded in mystery but it is believed to have been founded in the 11th century by the architect-priest Mpu Kuturan. Five hundred years later, the temple was rebuilt by the reformer-priest Dang Hyang Nirartha, who was the founder of the Shaivite presthood in Bali. Nirartha chose Pura Uluwatu as his last earthly abode.

Part of the temple fell into the sea just before the *puputan* (ritual suicide) of the royal court of Badung after the Dutch invasion of 1906 *(p55)*. This was regarded as an omen of the impending disaster. In the late 1990s, some of the shrines were set on fire by lightning, which was interpreted to augur the economic and political troubles of the time.

Until the beginning of the 20th century, admission to the temple was forbidden to anyone except for the princes of Badung. Visitors should cover their shoulders and knees; sarongs and sashes can be rented for a nominal fee.

↑ Hindu pilgrims gathering at Pura Luhur Uluwatu for a ceremony of prayers and worship

Did You Know?

The temple is sacred to fishers, who come to pray to the sea goddess, Dewi Laut.

↑ Pura Luhur Uluwatu, commanding a glorious position on a cliff top

Layout of the Temple

The inner sanctuaries of the temple are off limits to those who are not praying. However, much can be seen from the outside. The extremely hard, grey coral walls have enabled the temple and its well-preserved decorative stone carvings to survive for centuries. The outermost gate is a *candi bentar* or split gate whose inner sides are tipped with carved wings. This gate marks the spot where the human realm meets that of the gods.

The temple's layout follows the tripartite pattern of godly, human and demonic worlds in the form of three courtyards. Towering over the central courtyard is an enormous arched gate guarded by statues of the elephant-headed god, Ganesha – the remover of obstacles and the god of knowledge. Kala's monstrous face peers out from above the gate, while his hands reach out beside his head to catch any evil spirits foolish enough to attempt to sneak in. As the creator of light and a leader in the underworld, Kala's role is to balance unequal forces. Behind the main pagoda of the temple's small inner sanctum, a limestone statue of a Brahman priest, believed to be Dang Hyang Nirartha, surveys the Indian Ocean.

INSIDER TIP
Visiting

The best time to visit the temple is the late afternoon when the sea breezes rise. Monkeys inhabit this area so keep your valuables out of sight. A Kecak dance performance is held in the temple grounds at sunset every day.

Three-tiered meru

→
Illustration of the Pura Luhur Uluwatu, perched on a cliff top

The inner courtyard is reserved for worshippers.

↑ Guardian statue of Hanuman, a mythical Hindu monkey figure

These stepped paths along the cliff rise 200 m (650 ft) above the sea.

Candi bentar (split gate) forming the main entrance to the temple

The unusual arched main gate has the shape of Meru, the Cosmic Mountain of Hinduism. Surmounting it are three finials and a Kala head – a fanged demon with bulging eyes, believed to ward off evil spirits.

The arched stone gate leading to the inner courtyard

These Ganesha – elephant-headed guardian statues, wearing a belt with a clasp in the form of a Cyclops – are masterpieces of Balinese sculpture.

The jero tengah, or central courtyard, offers spectacular views of the sunset.

At the top of the stairs leading to the temple is a candi bentar (split gate), decorated with elaborate carvings.

The astasai is a shrine for festival offerings.

This shrine is dedicated to Dang Hyang Nirartha, with images of Brahma and Vishnu.

The bale tajuk are shrines for the spiritual guardians of Nirartha.

②

DENPASAR

▲ E4 🚌 **From Kuta, Sanur and Nusa Dua** 🛈 **Jalan Raya Puputan 41, Renon; (0361) 235 600**

Denpasar is Bali's bustling provincial capital. Some older buildings predate the Dutch invasion of 1906 (*p55*), and there are still some white-walled, red-tiled structures from colonial times. On the streets are several statues of key figures in Indonesia's struggle for independence. Around the main street, Jalan Gajah Mada, are shop-houses built by Chinese, Arab and Indian traders.

①

Pasar Badung

📍 **Jalan Gajah Mada**
🕐 **Daily**

Bali's oldest market, Pasar Badung is full of colour and excitement; sellers from all over Bali do a brisk trade all day. The extensive flower section is not to be missed – blossoms used in religious offerings (*p46*) are a major commodity on Bali.

The fruit, vegetable and fish market, which is in full swing from 6am to noon, is full of spectacular tropical harvests. Bargains can be found among the stalls offering textiles, mats, baskets and traditional dancers' costumes.

②

Kumbasari Art Market

📍 **Jalan Gajah Mada** 🕐 **5am–5pm daily**

Located just across the river from Pasar Badung, this four-storey rabbit warren of small shops specializes in handicrafts, souvenirs, artifacts, clothes, fabrics, gold work and other artistic goods.

The ground floor sells spices, ceremonial pots and jars, baskets and temple offerings. The first floor is dedicated to budget clothing, traditional textiles and random handicrafts. Art shops featuring handicrafts from Lombok, as well as Balinese

woodcarvings, can be found on the second floor. Check out the art shop on the mezzanine between the second and third floor, where the paintings are very reasonably priced. The third floor features more art shops, and on the fourth floor you'll find internationally designed products.

③

Jalan Gajah Mada

Several interesting Chinese apothecaries with an array of herbal medicines can be found on this busy street. One of the largest is Toko Saudara. Other stores sell electronics, sporting goods, handicrafts, batik and *ikat* textiles. Many traders of Arab and Indian descent have businesses here.

💬 **INSIDER TIP**
Tranquil Escape

Although a hectic city, Denpasar has quieter leafy streets in the Renon business district. The Bajra Sandhi Monument, commemorating the island's struggle against the Dutch, offers panoramic views.

Fruit and spice stalls at the sprawling Pasar Badung market

④ Taman Puputan

🏛 Jalan Udayana and Jalan Surapati

Puputan translates as "suicidal fight to the end", and this large square in the middle of town (once the site of Denpasar's palace) has a huge bronze statue which commemorates the *puputan* of the rajahs against the Dutch invaders of 1906 (*p55*). The monument portrays a Balinese family brandishing weapons. The woman holds jewels as the royal Balinese women are said to have thrown their jewellery at the Dutch soldiers in protest.

Did You Know?

Denpasar means "north market", reflecting its origins as a market town.

Nowadays the square is much more peaceful, making a pleasant green oasis amid the bustle and noise of Denpasar.

⑤ Catur Muka

🏛 Northwest corner of Taman Puputan

At the intersection of four streets, on the traffic island adjacent to Taman Puputan, is a representation of Brahma, the four-headed Hindu god of creation, who is shown in the form of a stone statue 20 m (65 ft) tall, dating from the 1970s. The name means "four faces". The landmark statue was created by the famous artist I Gusti Nyoman Lempad.

Bali Museum

⌂ Jalan Mayor Wisnu 1, on east side of Taman Puputan ☎ (0361) 222 680 ◷ 8am-4pm Mon-Thu, 8am-12:30pm Fri ✗ Public hols

The Bali Museum is the oldest on the island, and has more than 10,000 exhibits in several pavilions. There are archaeological finds dating back to the megalithic period, dance masks, textiles woven in the Bali Aga villages, crafts, ceremonial objects and displays on Bali's architectural styles and theatrical arts. The exterior walls, decorative split gates and courtyards have been structured in the classic Denpasar palace style, while the Tabanan (theatrical masks and musical instruments), Karangasem (sculptures, woodcarvings and paintings) and Buleleng (textiles) pavilions are built in the style of the regencies after which they are named.

Ignore the advances of unofficial guides and work your own way around the museum buildings. Most displays are labelled in English.

SHOPPING IN DENPASAR

Jalan Sulawesi is Denpasar's fabric street, devoted to cloth of all descriptions. Most of the stores are long and narrow lock-ups, open at the front, dimly lit and piled high with hundreds of rolls of cloth. Try to shake off the commission hunters who will latch on to you and offer to be your guide. Jalan Hasanudin is the locale for Bali's gold shops, featuring Balinese gold jewellery. If you change your mind after your purchase, most of the shops will allow you to return the item (supported by the guarantee certificate) and to get your money back, less 5–10 per cent. Most shops open daily from 9am until 9pm.

Pura Jagatnatha

⌂ Taman Puputan, Jalan Letkol Wisnu ◷ Daily

This temple was built in the 1970s for the worship of Sang Hyang Widhi Wasa, the Supreme God. It is crowded on the full and new moons, and on Kajeng Kliwon, an auspicious day for cleansing the mind, which falls every 15 days in the Balinese calendar. The temple has a tall *padmasana* ("lotus throne") shrine with an empty seat at the top open to the sky.

Pura Maospahit

⌂ Jalan Sutomo, Grenceng ✗ To the public

Dating to the 13th–15th centuries, when the Majapahit ruled over Bali (p54), this temple was badly damaged in an earthquake in 1917 and has been heavily restored since. The style of the statuary, the red brickwork and the restrained ornamentation developed during the Majapahit period are delightful. Although the temple is closed to visitors, the interesting architecture can be admired from outside.

Jalan Hasanudin

Shops selling a vast selection of gold jewellery in Balinese, Indonesian and Western designs line this street.

Jalan Sulawesi

This three-block stretch houses myriad fabrics and textiles. Everything from cheap batiks to imported silks and brocades can be found here. This is where the Balinese come to buy their temple clothing, and the delicate lace used for *kebaya* (a traditional tight-fitting ladies' blouse).

Taman Werdhi Budaya

🏛 Jalan Nusa Indah
📞 (0361) 227 176 🕐 8am-3:30pm Tue-Thu, Sat & Sun (to 1pm Fri) 🚫 Public hols

Also known as the Bali Arts Centre, this is an attractive if under-used complex. It has

gardens, an art museum, several indoor theatres and an outdoor amphitheatre. There are frequent dance and music performances, but no set programme.

The centre is a good place to come to during the heat of the day. Its permanent collection of sculptures and paintings reflects the art world of the 1970s and 1980s, and more recent works are shown in rotating exhibitions.

Information and events can be found listed in the *Bali Post* newspaper and tourist magazines.

Pemecutan Palace

🏛 Jalan Thamrin 25
📞 (0361) 423 491

Resting in the thick of the old city, Pemecutan Palace was the first of Denpasar's royal houses to open its doors to visitors. It is still inhabited by the current king of Denpasar.

← The tall lotus throne shrine in the Pura Jagatnatha temple

↑ Shop selling a wide range of textiles on Jalan Sulawesi

The palace has ornate and classic architecture and beautiful royal family shrines dating back to the 17th century. It consists of two main compounds – the living quarters and the place of worship. In the spacious outer courtyard there is a bell-tower and a gamelan pavilion. An elaborately carved gate leads to the middle courtyard, which is home to a *balairung*, or large hall, where the king still holds court, and there is an open stage for dance and theatre peformances.

↑ Detail of a sculpture in the grounds of Pemecutan Palace

3

SANUR

🗺 E4 🚌🚐 From Denpasar, Candi Dasa, Kuta, Lovina, Padang Bai, and Ubud ℹ Denpasar; (0361) 754 092

Bali's longest-established resort, Sanur has a simple layout and tranquil atmosphere that appeal to those seeking a relaxed holiday with the convenience and facilities of a beach resort.

Pura Desa

📍 Jalan Hang Tuah ⏰ Daily

This fine village temple was probably built early in the 20th century, although its brickwork has been restored since. It is in Sanur's oldest neighbourhood, which is famous for the spiritual power of its priests.

Pura Blanjong

📍 Jalan Danau Poso ⏰ Daily

In this plain-looking temple is an ancient stone column, the Prasasti Blanjong. On it is carved the oldest edict so far found in Bali (AD 914). The inscription is written in a form of Sanskrit, although it is not all decipherable. It suggests Sanur was a lively trading port more than 1,000 years ago.

Sanur Beach

The beach runs almost the full length of the town; along much of it is a paved walk. Offshore, enormous breakers crash into a reef. The calm waters between the reef and the white sands are good for swimming except at low tide and are excellent for exploring marine life. Beyond the reef

↑ The Pura Blanjong temple, housing a stone Sanskrit column

the currents are strong. Activities include diving, fishing trips and an evening sail on a *jukung*, a traditional outrigger.

Beach Promenade

A well-maintained paved promenade, including a 5-km (3-mile) cycle path,

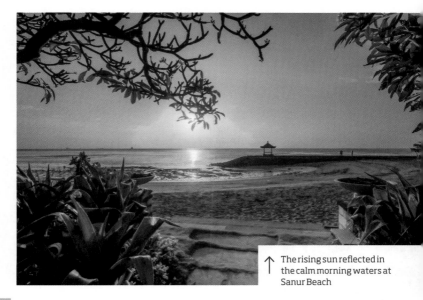

↑ The rising sun reflected in the calm morning waters at Sanur Beach

runs next to the sandy beach, saved from erosion by an impressive landscaping and conservation project that has also safeguarded the coral reef. Curved stone jetties extend at intervals, each with a bale pavilion on the end where fishers linger. The promenade is also home to two art markets, while the northern end marks the departure point for boats to Nusa Lembongan and Nusa Penida.

EAT

Fisherman's Club

Part of the Andaz Bali hotel, Fisherman's Club is an upscale take on the classic beachfront barbecue joint. Soak up the sea views here, while chowing down on fresh seafood.

🏠 Jalan Danau Tamblingan 89a
🌐 hyatt.com

Kayumanis Seaside Restaurant

This gem offers an exceptional menu of Western and Asian fusion dishes. Reservations recommended.

🏠 Jalan Pantai Sindhu
🌐 kayumanissanur.com

Naga Eight

Enjoy Cantonese dishes in an open-air setting – think coral walls and towering columns – in the very heart of Sanur.

🏠 Jalan Danau Tamblingan 89
🌐 nagaeight.com

---

⑤

Pura Segara

🏠 Jalan Segara Ayu, or from Sanur Beach ⏰ Daily

Set in the grounds of Segara Village Hotel, but accessible to the public, this is one of the best of several beach temples built of coral. The pyramid shape of the offering houses is unique to Sanur, suggesting origins in prehistoric times.

---

⑥

Museum Le Mayeur

🏠 Jalan Hang Tuah, via Grand Inna Bali Beach Hotel 📞 (0361) 286 201 ⏰ 8am–3:30pm daily (to 12:30pm Fri)

Built in the 1930s by Adrien-Jean Le Mayeur, a Belgian painter and one of Sanur's first European residents, the house became a museum and gallery on the artist's death in 1958. About 80 of Le Mayeur's paintings are on display. Many depict a colourful, idealized portrayal of Balinese life. Le Mayeur's wife, the Balinese dancer Ni Polok, is the subject of several paintings.

---

⑦

Duta Orchid Garden

🏠 Jalan Bypass Tohpati, Kasamba 1 ⏰ 8am–6pm daily 🌐 dutaorchid garden.com

This beautiful botanical garden is a serene tropical haven, with a huge variety of orchids that bloom throughout the year. For those keen to take home a piece of paradise, many of the flowers are also available to buy.

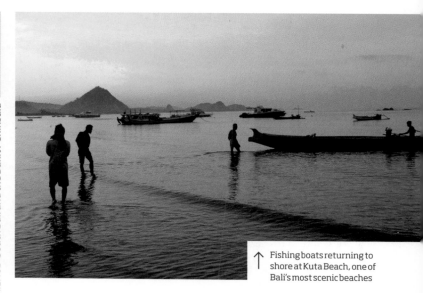

↑ Fishing boats returning to shore at Kuta Beach, one of Bali's most scenic beaches

KUTA AND LEGIAN

E4, 🚌 ℹ️ Jalan Raya Kuta and Jalan Pantai Kuta 2; (0361) 754 092

Wonderfully loud and busy, with a world-famous resort strip, Kuta and Legian are the most developed visitor destinations in Bali. The streets are lined with hotels, bars, restaurants, cafés, nightclubs and shops, while the long and sandy beach is popular with surfers. Besides the beach and water sports, the principal attractions are shopping and nightlife.

① Kuta and Legian Beach

The beach is flat and sandy, and stretches for over 3 km (2 miles), backed by some sizeable hotels. Hawkers sell their wares and refreshments are available all day long. Surfboards can be rented – this is a good place for the novice surfer, although you should watch out for the rip tides. Because of currents, swimmers should stay between the safety flags. Kuta Beach becomes Legian Beach north of Jalan Melasti.

Extending north from Kuta Beach, Legian Beach is a lovely stretch of white sand and has a slightly more relaxed ambience than Kuta. Legian's labyrinth of backstreets offers a wide range of family-friendly accommodation options close to the beach.

② Poppies Lanes I & II

These two narrow lanes are lined with small shops, stalls, hotels and bars. One of the first hotels to open in Kuta was Poppies, from which the lanes took their name. The network of alleys in this part of Kuta offers a refuge from the traffic, pollution and noise of the main streets.

③ Jalan Legian

This is the commercial artery of Kuta, running parallel with the beach. At the southern end is Bemo Corner, a busy intersection. The street connects Kuta and Seminyak. Jalan Legian is lined with

Did You Know?

Tourism in Bali began on Kuta Beach in the 1930s.

restaurants, surf stores, art shops, fashion boutiques and massage and reflexology parlours. One of Bali's primary nightlife hubs, the street is full of pubs, bars and nightclubs – some, such as The Bounty, Vi Ai Pi and Sky Garden Rooftop Lounge nightclubs, are landmarks in themselves.

---

④ Bali Bombing Memorial

 Jalan Legian, Kuta

This elegant stone monument is dedicated to those who lost their lives in the terrorist attack in Kuta on 12 October 2002. Built on the site of the destroyed Paddy's Pub, it has a marble plaque bearing the nationalities and names of the 202 victims. The fatalities included 88 Australians, 38 Indonesians and 23 British, as well as victims from 19 other countries. An additional 209 people were injured. The first bomb was detonated at Paddy's Pub at 11:05pm, causing patrons to flee the building; 20 seconds later, a powerful car bomb exploded outside the Sari Club on the opposite side of the street.

---

⑤ Kuta Square

 9am–10pm daily

Bali's original shopping arcade consists of a hotch-potch of glass-fronted shops, including a Matahari department store, a jewellery emporium, a large, high-end batik outlet, souvenir shops, local designer boutiques and sports shops. Surfwear concept stores include Dreamland Surf, Kuta Lines, Quiksilver, Volcom, Rip Curl and Billabong. Prominent international outlets such as Armani, Gucci, Versace and Donna Karan can also be found here. There is some speculation as to whether or not all of the designer goods are the genuine article, but price is usually the best guideline. There is also a good range of restaurants.

EAT

Poppies Restaurant
A Kuta institution, Poppies serves exquisite seafood and Indonesian and inter-national cuisine among flowers and waterfalls.

 Poppies Lane 1/19, Jalan Legian, Kuta
Ⓦ poppiesbali.com

⑭⑭⑭

Rosso Vivo Dine & Lounge
This delightful Italian restaurant, with ocean views and comfortable lounge seating, serves a wide range of pizzas, pastas and desserts.

Jalan Pantai Kuta, Kuta Ⓦ rossovivo bali.com

⑭⑭⑭

Made's Warung
Established in 1969, this is the most famous restaurant in Kuta. It serves Indonesian, Western, Thai and Japanese cuisine.

Jalan Pantai Kuta, Banjar Pande Mas, Kuta
Ⓦ madeswarung. com/kuta

 ⑭⑭⑭

> **Extending north from Kuta Beach, Legian Beach is a lovely stretch of white sand and has a slightly more relaxed ambience than Kuta.**

EXPERIENCE MORE

EAT

CRATE

A popular open-air coffee shop, boutique, and art gallery, this is where Canggu's residents and visitors come to see and be seen.

🅰D4 🏠Jalan Canggu Padang Linjong 49, Canggu 🌐lifes crate.com

Queen's Tandoor

High-quality Indian cuisine here includes tandoori dishes, curries and biryanis.

🅰E4 🏠Jalan Kartika Plaza, South Kuta 🌐bali.queens tandoor.com

Taco Beach Grill

The delightful Taco Beach Grill serves innovative California-style Mexican food, fused with Balinese dishes such as *babi guling* burritos.

🅰E4 🏠Jalan Kunti I 8, Seminyak 🌐taco beachgrill.com

Mama San

Asian comfort food is served in this hip restaurant with a Shanghai 1920s-era vibe.

🅰E4 🏠Jalan Raya Kerobokan 135, Seminyak 🌐mamasanbali.com

⑤ 🍴 🖥 🛍
South Kuta Beach

🅰E4 🚌From Kuta 🛈Kuta; (0361) 754 092

The South Kuta Beach area (also known as Tuban) stretches south from Kuta Square along Jalan Kartika Plaza, towards the airport boundary. Land reclamation projects have restored the beach to its former glory, and massive investments have resulted in upgrades and renovations to provide elegant accommodation and world-class facilities just steps from the sand. This family-oriented area provides a broad choice of international accommodation options, ranging from simple home-stays to mid-range hotels and five-star resorts, many of which have multiple dining venues, swanky rooftop bars and luxurious spas.

The white sandy beach has a 3-km (2-mile) boardwalk, which is great for strolling, jogging or cycling, in between stopping off at the many shops, restaurants and cafés. Visitors can enjoy an eclectic array of restaurants offering a variety of cuisines, as well as the popular beachfront Discovery Mall and Lippo Mall with its three-theatre

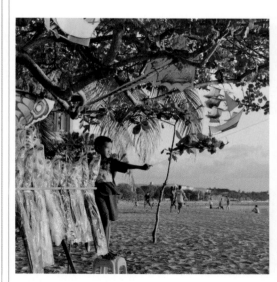

↑ A boy playing with the wares at his father's kite stall on South Kuta Beach

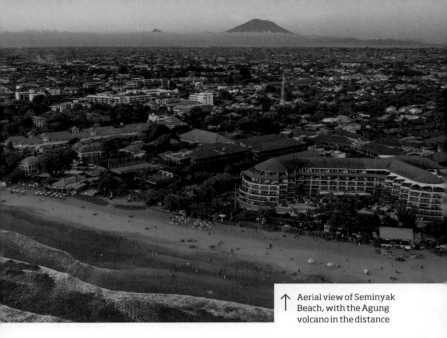

↑ Aerial view of Seminyak Beach, with the Agung volcano in the distance

Cinemaxx complex, which presents daily screenings of the latest Hollywood blockbusters. Both of these modern shopping malls are air-conditioned, providing a welcome respite from the heat. There is also a superb selection of independent shops, as well as the Kuta Art Market on Jalan Bakung Sari, plenty of indulgent day spas, and numerous bars and nightlife venues offering live music, cabaret shows and the opportunity to dance the night away. Family recreation options include **Waterbom Bali**, featuring a whole host of exhilarating waterslides that will get the heart racing, as well as a children's area, a lazy river, massage facilities, restaurants and shady cabanas surrounded by tropical gardens.

The beach is the departure point for surfers wishing to make their way to the break at Kuta Reef; fishers with motorized outriggers can be chartered for the trip.

Waterbom Bali

⊗ ⓨ ⊜ 🅰 Jalan Kartika Plaza Tuban ⓦ waterbombali.com

6 ⓨ ⊜ 🛍

Seminyak

🅰 E4 🚌 From Kuta 🚕 Kuta; (0361) 754 092

Seminyak extends north of Kuta and Legian. The further north you go, the more peaceful the atmosphere becomes, although Seminyak is a dynamic, major tourist hub. Some good fashion boutiques can be found here, selling stylish clothes made in the region.

The luxurious Oberoi Hotel has lovely gardens overlooking the beach. Further north still, in the Petitenget area, you'll find Potato Head Beachclub, with three bars, three restaurants and an infinity pool , and the glamorous W Retreat, which has pools restaurants and a spa.

A short walk up the beach north of Seminyak is the **Pura Petitenget** ("magic chest") temple, raised some 8 m (26 ft) above road level. Founded by the 16th-century priest Dang Hyang Nirartha, who was the founder of the Shaivite priesthood in Bali, it is one of a series of sea

temples stretching from Pura Luhur Uluwatu on the Bukit Peninsula north to Pura Tanah Lot in Western Bali. Considered one of Bali's most mystically charged temples, it is the site of many important ceremonies.

The area from Seminyak to Kerobokan, 5 km (3 miles) to its north, is a furniture-making centre. Galleries line the main road.

Pura Petitenget

⊗ 🅰 Jalan Kayu Aya 🕐 Daily

SUNSETS IN SEMINYAK

A popular activity around Seminyak is to gather on the beach in the evening to watch the stunning sunsets of reds, oranges and purples while sipping a cold beer. A good place for this magical experience is the stretch of sand near Pura Petitenget, which tends to be less busy than the main beach.

7

Canggu

 D4 ℹ Denpasar; (0361) 756176

A 12-km (seven-mile) drive northwest of Seminyak on the edge of the Badung greenbelt, the villages of Tibubeneng, Berawa, Canggu and Pererenan – collectively known as Canggu – used to be little more than a sleepy coastal district celebrated among the surfing fraternity for its beach breaks. The advent in 2006, however, of the international Canggu Community School led to the area drawing in a more family-oriented and affluent ex-pat community, with real-estate developers competing for the most cherished plots of land.

Canggu has since evolved into Bali's hippest beachside scene, popular for its juice bars, coffee shops, numerous restaurants, and vegan cafés promoting healthy cuisine.

Exercise fanatics can choose between three fitness clubs, a dance studio, copious yoga centres and a couple of surf schools. Finn's Recreation Club offers sports and leisure facilities, including Splash kids' waterpark. Horse lovers who relish a canter along the beach will find three riding stables in the area, while a pulsating nightlife scene can be enjoyed at Canggu's live-music venues.

Other attractions include spas and beauty lounges, fashion boutiques and two beach clubs. Accommodation ranges from opulent holiday villas, beachside resorts and surf camps, to yoga retreats, serviced apartments, eco-hotels and guesthouses. Meanwhile, traditional Balinese village life continues in Canggu as it has always done. Crops are planted and harvested, ritual music is carried on the breeze and temple ceremonies are a common sight.

Did You Know?

In 2018, Canggu was named the fastest-growing beach destination in the world.

STAY

Padma Resort Legian

Set amid lush tropical gardens, this five-star resort dominates a prime beachfront location in Legian's heart.

E4 ⬛ Jalan Padma 1, Legian 🌐 padmaresort legian.com

Gravity Boutique Hotel

Surfers will love this boho-chic eco-resort near Bingin and Padang Padang.

D5 ⬛ Jalan Labuan Sait, South Kuta 🌐 gravitybalihotel.com

Grün Canggu

This treehouse hotel has six elevated studio apartments named after Bali's endemic trees.

D4 ⬛ Jalan Veteran 87, Buduk 🌐 grunresorts.com

Surfers heading into the water at a popular spot on Canggu Beach

Pulau Serangan

▲E4

The island of Serangan is separated from the southern curve of Sanur Beach by a mangrove area known as Suwungwas. It is also known as "Turtle Island" due to being a nesting ground for green sea turtles. The island has been greatly extended and its natural landscape changed by reclamation during construction work for the Kura Kura Bali development. A causeway links it to mainland Bali. The two original old fishing villages of Ponjok and Dukuh remain. Besides the Balinese Hindus, there is an old Bugis Muslim community whose ancestors migrated here from South Sulawesi in the 1600s.

Pulau Serangan is home to one of the six most sacred temples in Bali – **Pura Sakenan**, located on the westernmost edge of the

island. The temple is said by some to have been founded by the 16th-century reformist priest Dang Hyang Nirartha. Others, however, believe the temple was founded in the 11th century by the Javanese Buddhist priest Mpu Kuturan. Within the inner courtyard is a stepped pyramid built of white coral, reminiscent of temples in Polynesia. During Galungan (p52), a vibrant festival takes place here every 210 days on the temple's anniversary, drawing huge numbers of devotees.

The island is good for watersports, especially surfing on its eastern side. It is also a good vantage point from which to watch vessels returning to Benoa Harbour at the end of the day. There are great views of Nusa Dua, Nusa Lembongan and Nusa Penida islands and beautiful sunsets.

Pura Sakenan
◈ 🏠 Pulau Serangan
🕙 Daily

Benoa Harbour

▲C4 🚌 From Denpasar (shuttle bus services to Benoa from hotels) 🚢 To Lembar on Lombok

Linked to Nusa Dua by a scenic highway across the Benoa Bay, Benoa Harbour will appeal to boat-lovers. Among the commercial and privately owned vessels, there is often an interesting variety of traditional craft from the Indonesian archipelago. These include pinisi, broad-beamed sailing cargo boats from South Sulawesi; and brightly coloured fishing boats from Madura, off northeast Java. There is a multitude of boat charters and tours on offer. Day trips to Nusa Lembongan (p89) are recommended, while longer excursions can be taken as far as Komodo and the Lesser Sunda Islands.

Nearby, on the Jalan Bypass Ngurah Rai, is the Mangrove Information Centre (0361 726 969), which aims to preserve the 15 species of coastal mangrove in its natural forest.

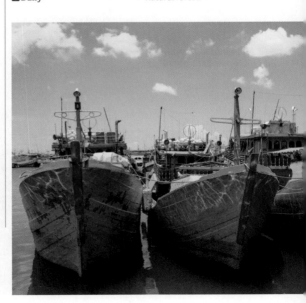

→
Balinese fishing boats lined up in Benoa Harbour

EAT

Sundara Bali

This refined beach club becomes a sophisticated restaurant by night offering sushi, Wagyu steaks and seafood.

⚠E4 ☐Four Seasons Resort, Jalan Bukit Permai, Jimbaran
🌐sundarabali.com

The Shady Shack

Enjoy healthy, meat-free dishes at this shabby-chic, roadside shack.

⚠D4 ☐Jalan Tanah Barak 57, Canggu
📞(0819) 1639 5087

Cuca

Globally inspired dishes from local ingredients include enticing tapas, fun cocktails and creative desserts.

⚠E4 ☐Jalan Yoga Perkanthi, Jimbaran
🌐cucabali.com

Nelayan Restaurant

Set in a thatched pavilion, Nelayan serves fresh seafood platters with a Mediterranean influence.

⚠E4 ☐Jalan Yoga Perkhanti, Jimbaran
📞(0361) 701 605

Seafood Cafés

More than 30 seafood cafés line the beach at Jimbaran Bay, offering grilled feasts.

⚠E4 ☐Pantai Jimbaran

Tanjung Benoa

⚠E4 🚌From Nusa Dua
ℹKuta; (0361) 754 092

Tanjung (meaning "Cape") Benoa is a long, narrow, sandy spit, with a small fishing village built on it. The cape is separated from Benoa Harbour by a narrow stretch of water. The village was once a trading port, and some Chinese and Bugis as well as Balinese still live here. There are several Balinese temples built of carved limestone, and a mosque. At the ancient bright-red Caow Eng Bio Chinese temple, built by sailors and traders on the northern end of the peninsula, fishers of all religions regularly consult with the fortune-teller in the hope of finding a good catch.

A modern road leads to the tip of the peninsula from Nusa Dua. Hotels, spas and restaurants specializing in grilled seafood line both sides of the road. One quirky landmark is the stone pineapple motif marking the entrance to the Novotel.

A beach restoration project has resulted in a series of picturesque, crescent-shaped stone piers, complete with open-sided gazebos. There are facilities for water sports, such as water-skiing, banana boat rides, fishing and parasailing. Cruise operators offer trips out to sea for snorkelling in waters rich in corals and tropical fish.

Jimbaran

⚠E4 ℹKuta; (0361) 754 092

A large fishing village and resort, Jimbaran has one of Bali's best beaches. A beautiful arc of white sand lines its bay, which is protected by an unbroken coral reef. The beach is a great place to watch sunsets and has spectacular views. On a clear day the profiles of all Bali's volcanoes and hills are visible from here, including the three peaks of Gunung Batukaru to the west (p160), and Gunung Batur (p120), Gunung Agung (p142), Gunung Abang (p143) and Gunung Seraya (p141) to the east. The beach offers sailing boats for hire and the waves are good for bodysurfing.

A lively fish market takes place daily from early morning until mid-afternoon along the bay. The daily morning market on Jalan Uluwatu sells superb fresh produce.

The Chinese Buddhist Caow Eng Bio temple in Tanjung Benoa ↑

Fisherman casting a
fishing net off the coast
of Jimbaran at sunset ↑

Jimbaran offers a plethora of great places to eat, especially seafood restaurants. The beach is lined with thatch-roofed cafés, where diners choose their fresh seafood, which is then grilled over coconut husks and delivered to the table.

There are no individual buildings of great interest to visit in Jimbaran, but it is a good place for observing local everyday life. A large fishing settlement consisting of simple huts sits near the waterfront. Many of the fishers are not of Balinese origin, but migrants from the islands of Java and Madura. The brightly painted boats with their impressive bows and sterns can be seen all day long bobbing at anchor in the surf off the coast. As the sun begins to set, the fishing craft set off into the dusk with lamps burning – an unforgettable sight.

A little north of Jimbaran, Kuta Reef is one of Bali's best surfing points. The reef break is just one of the surfing spots in the sea around the Ngurah Rai International Airport and can be reached by chartering an outrigger at Jimbaran. South of Jimbaran, much of the coast is a series of limestone cliffs interspersed with some of Bali's most luxurious holiday rental villas and boutique hotels.

12

Garuda Wisnu Kencana Cultural Park

E5 **Jalan Raya Uluwatu, Ungasan** **8am–7:30pm daily** **gwkbali.com**

This hillside cultural park and event venue, also known simply as GWK, has as its centrepiece an immense statue, which is visible from a distance of 25 km (15 miles). The iconic statue cost US$30 million and was 28 years in the making. The 64-m (210-ft) wide structure sits atop a lofty pedestal that brings its total height to 121 m (397 ft), making it one of the largest monumental statues in the world. Sculpted in green copper and brass, it is a representation of the Hindu god Vishnu, riding on the back of Garuda, the winged messenger, as his trusted companion. Together, Garuda and Vishnu symbolize the harmony between humankind and the environment, as well as the spirituality of Bali.

The statue and park are the concept of the leading Indonesian sculptor Nyoman Nuarta, whose vision was to create an arena for culture and art. Shows of Indonesian and Balinese traditional dance and music take place daily. Venues include the Lotus Pond outdoor area, enclosed by enormous limestone pillars, the Street Theatre, Plaza Kura-Kura and Indraloka Garden. The complex also has a gallery for art exhibitions, a cinema, a restaurant serving Balinese cuisine and a gift shop with a range of souvenirs and handicrafts.

→

Bali's most iconic landmark,
the GWK statue depicting
the Hindu god Vishnu

Padang Padang Beach

D5 **Kuta; (0361) 754 092**

Locally known as Pantai Labuan Sait, Padang Padang is an archetypically enchanting beach nestled into a pocket of lava rocks, complete with a long stretch of golden sand. Located on the northwestern coast of the Bukit Peninsula beside a road bridge over a river, it is accessed via a flight of stairs through a cave crevice. The surf has a steady set of barrels during good weather and is the venue for international surfing events, of which the Rip Curl Cup Padang Padang is the most frequently held. The beach was made famous by the Hollywood movie *Eat Pray Love* starring Julia Roberts and Javier Bardem. Jalan Labuan Sait, the road that loops past the beach, is lined with surf

BALI'S SURF HISTORY

The 1960s saw the first surfers begin to arrive in Bali. They spoke of a "secret spot" on the southwestern tip – a place that would go on to become world-famous with the release of the 1971 surf movie *Morning of the Earth*. Meanwhile, a group of local Balinese youngsters broke through centuries-old beliefs that the sea was the home of demons. Using borrowed surfboards, they didn't take long to master the sport, although it would take them half a day to reach the spot where they thought the waves might be breaking. The lure of the surf has been deeply intertwined with the rise of tourism on Bali because the earliest guesthouses in Kuta were in fact built to accommodate visiting surfers.

camps, surf schools and surf shops, guesthouses, bungalow-style accommodation, cafés and local *warungs*, a boutique eco-resort and a five-star hotel. The whole area is characterized by a dry, rocky landscape dotted with stunted bush, cactus, kapok trees and wild flowers.

Pecatu

D5 **i** Kuta; (0361) 754 092

Pecatu is the district that covers the southwest Bukit Peninsula, from Balangan Beach and Dreamland Beach on the peninsula's north coast, to Uluwatu at the western tip and Nyang Nyang Beach in the south. Until the turn of the 21st century, this dry-land outcrop was home solely to seaweed farmers, fishers, cassava farmers and die-hard surfers. It is now the most upmarket destination on the island. The white-gold beaches here are among Bali's best, pounded by thrilling surf breaks. Party-goers will love the clifftop Omnia Dayclub, and golfers will enjoy the 18-hole, championship-standard New Kuta Golf Course at Kawasan Pecatu Indah Resort, both of which command splendid ocean views.

Bingin Beach

D4 **i** Kuta; (0361) 754 092

The white sand and pristine turquoise water of Bingin Beach is reached via a descent of hundreds of steep, crumbling steps, but you'll be rewarded with sensational views of the beautiful coastline and Indian Ocean as you zigzag past the rustic buildings that are set into the cliffs. When the tide is out, the beach is covered with fascinating rock pools. But when the tide is in, much of the beach vanishes, and you'll have to retreat to one of the many *warungs* that line the sand, from where you can watch Bingin's exceptional surf sets, rolling in, one after another. Close to the beach are plenty of homestays and cafés catering to the young surfing crowd.

TOP 5 EXPERIENCES ON THE BUKIT PENINSULA

Beer and Surf
Enjoy a Bintang beer at sunset at a clifftop *warung* in Uluwatu (p86) while watching the fearless surfers performing their moves on the waves below.

Spa Relaxation
A two-hour session in the Thermes Marins Bali Aquatonic Pool at Ayana Resort & Spa (www.ayana.com) is an unforgettable journey through therapeutic jetstreams.

Fire Dance
Watch an exciting Kecak fire-dance performance at sunset at the clifftop amphitheatre in the grounds of Uluwatu Temple (from 6pm daily; p68).

Hit the Clubs
Relax on the beach or party on the cliff top at one of the Bukit Peninsula's opulent beach clubs or day clubs.

Beach Trek
Get off the beaten track by descending 535 steps to the gorgeous, pristine white-sand Nyang Nyang Beach and relish the seclusion.

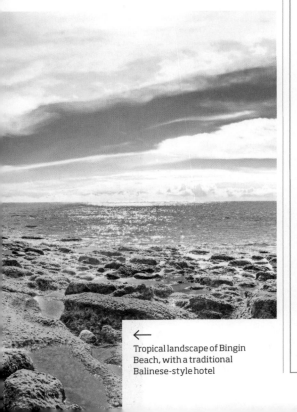

← Tropical landscape of Bingin Beach, with a traditional Balinese-style hotel

16

Uluwatu

D5

Bali's surf hotspot, Uluwatu is the most popular surf destination on the Bukit Peninsula due to its world-famous surf breaks. The area has many beach clubs and clifftop day clubs with swimming pools, sunloungers and fine restaurants. Many clifftop *warungs* offer views of the surf, cold beers and local dishes such as *nasi goreng* and fried noodles.

DRINK

Single Fin

With a huge balcony overlooking Uluwatu's surf break, this clifftop surfer-friendly spot packs in the crowds for post-beach beers.

D5 Pantai Suluban, Jalan Labuan Sait, Uluwatu
W singlefinbali.com

Ji Terrace by the Sea

Set on Canggu beach, this upscale bar is well-known for its pan-Asian fusion cocktails, wide choice of Japanese sake and regular DJ nights. Come early to nab a spot.

D4 Jalan Pantai Batu Bolong, Canggu
W jirestaurantbali.com

Delpi Rock Lounge

Perched on a cliff, this café-bar offers superb views of the beach.

D5 Jalan Uluwatu, Pecatu (0878) 6001 6022

Plentiful accommodation ranges from glamorous private estates, holiday villas and internationally branded boutique hotels to humble homestays. Despite its hipster vibe and a booming bar, café and restaurant culture, Uluwatu still retains a more laidback atmosphere than Kuta and Seminyak.

Access to Suluban Beach is via a steep concrete staircase through a narrow crag in a cliff. The beautiful beach is characterized by luminescent aquamarine water surrounded by limestone caves and cliffs. The best time to visit is during low tide, which reveals small caves and tidal pools that offer a pleasurable soak. Be sure to watch the tides, though, because the currents are strong, and waves can crash through cave openings. From here, surfers paddle out to the reef – this destination is for advanced or expert surfers only.

The area is also famous for the Pura Luhur Uluwatu temple (p66). Fascinating Kecak dance performances take place daily at 6pm at the open amphitheatre next to the temple against a glorious sunset.

↑ Surfers entering the waters at Uluwatu between the cliffs

17

Ungasan

E5

From Ungasan village's central position, 4 km (2.5 miles) from the Garuda Wisnu Kencana Cultural Park (p83) on the Bukit Peninsula, the Ungasan district extends to Bali's southernmost cliff, incorporating Karma Beach Club, Sunday's Beach Club, Banyan

→ Sun loungers and umbrellas at a luxury beach resort in Nusa Dua

Tree Resort, Melasti Beach and the isolated Green Bowl Beach. There is no coast road, so although these places are close to each other as the crow flies, they are a fair distance apart via narrow winding lanes. Green Bowl is reached via a 300-step descent. At low tide, the calm, clear waters allow for great snorkelling, while the surf waves are a short paddle beyond a natural reef barrier.

Nusa Dua

⚑E4 ⌖ 🛈Denpasar; (0361) 225 649

The Nusa Dua (literally "Two Islands") area is named after the two peninsulas along its coast. Built in the 1970s, the gated complex at Nusa Dua, for which the area is most famous, consists primarily of luxury resorts run by major hotel chains, and sandy beaches. The road leading to the entrance of the compound is lined with rows of statues; it leads through a large *candi bentar* (split gate), on each side of which carvings of frogs serve as guardian figures.

> Built in the 1970s, the gated complex at Nusa Dua, for which the area is most famous, consists primarily of luxury resorts run by major hotel chains, and sandy beaches

Inside is a calm atmosphere, away from the chaos of the rest of the island. The hotels are built on a big scale. Their grandiose entrances have been described as "Bali Baroque" or "expanded traditional" in style and are of interest to architecture enthusiasts. Young visitors will love the fish ponds of the Ayodya Resort, where thousands of brightly coloured *koi* (a type of carp first bred in Japan) swim among water lilies. The Bali National Golf Club has a championship course over three types of terrain (highland, coconut grove and coastal). Regular dance and other cultural activities are held at Nusa Dua.

Other facilities include the Bali International Convention Centre, the Bali Collection Mall, restaurants and the large **Pasifika Museum** housing a collection of artworks, including paintings, sculpture and textiles, from Asian Pacific cultures spanning several centuries. There are also 20th-century paintings by European artists who lived in Bali, including Arie Smit, Adrien-Jean Le Mayeur and Theo Maier.

Outside the gates of the Nusa Dua complex is the bustling village of Bualu. Several streets are lined with restaurants offering fresh fish and shops selling handicrafts.

Between the Sheraton Laguna and Grand Hyatt hotels, a headland with native flora and several Balinese shrines juts out into the sea. The views from here are splendid. South of Geger Beach is a path that leads up to Pura Geger, a small temple.

West of Nusa Dua, on the road to Uluwatu, is the Garuda Wisnu Kencana Cultural Park *(p83)*, which regularly stages exhibitions and performances.

Pasifika Museum
⊗ 🏠Area Block P, Nusa Dua
🕒10am–6pm daily
🌐museum-pasifika.com

Stone arch,
and *(inset)*
coral reef, on
the coast of
Nusa Penida

Nusa Penida

🅰F4 & G4 🚢From Sanur,
Kusamba & Padang Bai
ℹ️Klungkung; (0366) 21 448

This quiet but developing
island, once the penal colony of
the Raja of Klungkung, is the
legendary home of Ratu Gede
Mecaling, the Balinese "King
of Magical Powers". Here,
Balinese language and art
have been less subject to
change than on the mainland.
In general the landscape is
dry, even arid, resembling the
limestone hills of the Bukit
Peninsula. Towards the south
coast, with its tall white cliffs,
there are a few lusher hills.

Reached via a 30-minute
fastboat ride from Sanur,
Nusa Penida is ripe for
adventure and popular with
day-trippers. There are no
large resorts or fancy

restaurants here but a fair
number of homestays, budget
hotels and quality *warungs*,
most built on the north coast.
The northeast coast is home
to the gorgeous, remote
Atuh Beach. Much of the
west and south coast is only
accessible via potholed roads,
best carefully negotiated
on a motorcycle. Nevertheless, a treasure chest of epic
scenery awaits at Broken
Beach, Angel's Billabong
and Kelingking Beach, with
its breathtaking vista of a
golden-sand cove, reached via
a perilous cliff-face descent.

Some cotton is grown on
Nusa Penida. From it is woven
the *cepuk*, a form of *ikat*
textile (p136) thought to have
magical, protective powers.
Other local occupations
include seaweed farming.

There are several interesting
temples here. One is the
Pura Ped, in the village of

Toyapakeh. The temple is built
on an island in a large lotus
pond. Among the carvings in
Pura Kuning, near Semaya,
are some explicitly erotic
reliefs. The *pura desa*, or
village temple, of the inland
village of Batumadeg also
has some interesting decorative reliefs. They show sea
creatures, including crabs
and shellfish. The main gate
is especially imposing.

On the southwest coast,
Pura Gunung Cemeng is
a temple balanced atop a
pinnacle; from the neighbouring clifftops, you can see
graceful manta rays gliding
through the waters 200 m
(650 ft) below.

HIDDEN GEM
Atuh Beach

A blissful, hidden
crescent of white sand,
Nusa Penida's Atuh
Beach is accessible
via a steep stairway
or narrow tracks along
a rugged cliff face. It
offers café shacks,
sunbeds and umbrellas.

A short distance south of Suana is a sacred limestone cave, Goa Karangsari.

Nusa Penida is also a haven for rare birds. Here, the Friends of the National Parks Foundation (FNPF) has been repopulating species since 2004. This and riches such as hidden bathing pools and virgin rainforest await the intrepid explorer.

The waters off the coast are crystal-clear, but the currents can be strong. Here experienced divers will spot many rare underwater species. There are fine coral formations, especially off the south coast, where the sea is famed for spectacular giant sunfish; these shy creatures, weighing up to 1,000 kg (2,200 lb), might be spied from July to October. Sailfish and the whale shark can also occasionally be seen. Off the northern half of the island the clear waters are shallower and calmer, especially in the strait between Nusa Penida and Nusa Lembongan. Most people who dive off these islands make their arrangements with operators in Sanur.

Nusa Lembongan

A F4 From Sanur, Kusamba & Padang Bai Klungkung, Jalan Untung Surapati 3; (0366) 21 448

This small island has sandy beaches for sun-lovers and good coral reefs for divers and snorkellers. Bird-lovers will find a variety of species.

Day trips to the island have been available since the early 1990s. In operation now are several jet catamarans, the best known of them being the Bali Hai Cruises (www.balihaicruises.com); as a consequence the island is visited by larger groups than hitherto. Trips to the island are also offered by some local boat owners. The boats include *pinisi*, a type of Indonesian sailing vessel originating in the island of Sulawesi in northeast Indonesia.

Most boat operators rent watersports equipment, and snorkelling and diving gear.

On the island is an extensive underground house, known as the Cavehouse. It was dug by a Balinese priest after he was instructed in dreams to live in the belly of Mother Earth. He has passed away but the cave remains a popular curiosity.

For those who like pristine islands with no cars, Nusa Lembongan is a good place to stay a night or two. However, the best advice is to visit soon, because the island is developing quickly.

Nusa Ceningan

A F4

Linked to Nusa Lembongan by an iconic yellow suspension bridge, the tiny island of Nusa Ceningan is home to a small village of seaweed farmers. In the late afternoons you'll see their boats crowded around the plantations, reminiscent of a floating marketplace. Women are the main labourers; growth is fast and new shoots are harvested every 45 days. The produce is then dried and exported, mainly to Japan, for processing and use in cosmetics, food stabilizers and medicines. The natural sights of Ceningan are the stunning Blue Lagoon and Secret Beach, which is lapped by crystalline waters.

EAT

Tigerlillys
A tropical oasis in a hotel of the same name, Tigerlillys offers breakfast, snacks and a lunch and dinner menu. Highlights include acai bowls and *san choy bau* (lettuce wraps).

A F4 Jalan Jungutbatu, Jungutbatu, Nusa Lembongan tiger lillyslembongan.com

Sandy Bay Beach Club
This beachside restaurant with a pool offers an all-day menu of Asian and international selections.

A F4 Jalan Sandy Bay, Jungutbatu, Nusa Lembongan sandy baylembongan.com

Ogix Warung
Offering fabulous sea views from the cliff-side, this open-air restaurant serves classic local dishes.

A F4 Suana, Nusa Penida (0813) 3937 7892

CENTRAL BALI

Central Bali's broad slopes, with their terraced
rice fields and hundreds of villages, were the
cradle of traditional Balinese society. This area
encompasses the regency (and former kingdom)
of Gianyar, made up of many *puri* (noble houses)
whose former glory lives on in the courtly arts of
sculpture, painting, gold- and silversmithing,
music, dance and theatrical performance.

Between the Petanu and Pakrisan rivers are the
remains of one of Bali's oldest civilizations. From
the 9th to the 11th century, Bali was ruled by
Hindu-Buddhist kingdoms centred near present-
day Pejeng and Bedulu, a short distance from
Ubud. After the Majapahit seized Bali in the
14th century, power shifted to Klungkung but
it returned here in the 18th century. At that time
branches of the Klungkung dynasty grew into rival
kingdoms, two of which were based in Sukawati and
Gianyar. Satellite *puri* competed in architectural
and ritual display. Ubud became internationally
famous as a gateway into Bali's cultural heartland
when several western artists and intellectuals
settled here in the 1930s. As a major cultural and
artistic centre, it still attracts many visitors today.

CENTRAL BALI

Must Sees
- ❶ Bali Bird Park
- ❷ Ubud

Experience More
- ❸ Batubulan
- ❹ Bali Reptile Park
- ❺ Celuk
- ❻ Batuan
- ❼ Sukawati
- ❽ Blahbatuh
- ❾ Gianyar
- ❿ Bona
- ⓫ Bedulu
- ⓬ Mas
- ⓭ Goa Gajah
- ⓮ Peliatan
- ⓯ Pejeng
- ⓰ Ayung River Gorge
- ⓱ Kemenuh
- ⓲ Petulu
- ⓳ Tegallalang
- ⓴ Sebatu
- ㉑ Taro
- ㉒ Tampaksiring

CENTRAL BALI

Yangapi

Menanga

Rendang

Sekar

Unda

Gembalan

KLUNG-
KUNG

Akah

Besar

Tengading

Amuk Bay

Padang Bai

Gunaksa

Pesinggahan

Gelgel

Gelgel

Kusamba

Klotak

Jumpai

Badung
Strait

0 kilometres   3

0 miles   3

N

❶ 🔶 🔶 🍴 🖥 🛍

BALI BIRD PARK

📍 E4 🏠 Jalan Serma Cok Ngurah Gambir, Singapadu, Batubulan
🕐 9am–5:30pm daily 🚫 Nyepi 🌐 balibirdpark.com

Built on what was originally an expanse of rice fields, Bali Bird Park, or Taman Burung, is where visitors can see a profusion of birds from Indonesia, Latin America, Africa and Australia at close quarters.

There are almost 1,000 birds here, many of them in big, walk-in aviaries. The park is committed to the preservation, conservation and breeding of many endangered species, including more than 40 species of Indonesian birds. The areas in which the birds are kept recreate their natural habitats, complete with indigenous plantlife, including more than 300 trees and plants in a beautiful landscaped setting.

Bird Species

Among the 250 or so bird species in the Bird Park is the Australian pelican, a large waterbird that sometimes wanders as far as Indonesia, and the lesser bird of paradise from New Guinea, which has been hunted close to extinction. You can also see the Victoria crowned pigeon, one of the three crowned pigeon species from New Guinea, the Nicorbar pigeon, the pink-necked pigeon, the great argus pheasant, the African grey parrot, which can be trained to mimic, and the Asian pied hornbill with its distinct, loud, raucous call.

Species being bred here include Bali's only endemic bird, the endangered Bali starling (*Leucopsar rothschildi; p148*), as well as several species of parrots and coctakoos native to Indonesia and the attractive Australian Major Mitchell's cockatoo.

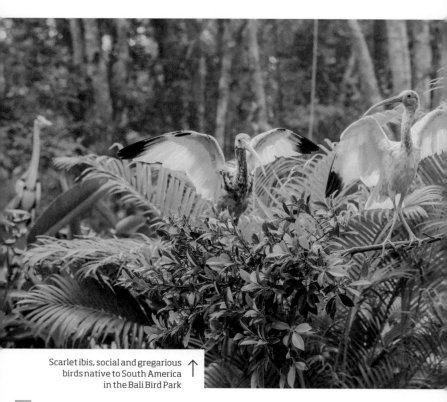

Scarlet ibis, social and gregarious birds native to South America in the Bali Bird Park ↑

1 Bali starlings, Bali's only surviving indigenous bird.

2 African crowned cranes.

3 Sun conures, vibrantly coloured parakeets native to South America.

Did You Know?

The scarlet ibis is the world's only red shorebird.

OWL HOUSE

Rarely seen in the wild, Indonesian owls, such as the buffy fish owl and the barred or Sumatran eagle owl, are a highlight of the Bali Bird Park and are housed in the Toraja House, a typical house from Sulawesi. There are 38 recognized species of Indonesian owl. Their secretive nature and, in some cases, inhospitable habitats, are reasons why little is known about them.

← Buffy fish owl, which lives near water and eats fish

↑ Pura Taman Saraswati temple, set in a water garden full of lotus plants

 2

UBUD

 E3 🚌 From Denpasar & Kuta ℹ️ Jalan Raya Ubud; (0361) 973 285

Bali's cultural and artistic heart, Ubud has long been known as the "village of painters". In the 1930s, many international artists and intellectuals came here to capture the "real Bali". Today, it is packed with art studios, galleries and shops selling an array of crafts.

①

Pura Taman Saraswati

🏛️ Jalan Kajen, off Jalan Raya Ubud ⏰ Daily

This temple was built in the 1950s by the Balinese stone sculptor and architect I Gusti Nyoman Lempad at the command of Ubud's prince, in honour of Saraswati, the Hindu deity of learning and the arts. A fine example of classical Balinese temple architecture, it is set in a water garden, with a lotus pond as the centrepiece. The temple has fine carvings by Lempad: a 3-m (10-ft) statue of the demon Jero Gede Mecaling; and the *padmasana* shrine in the northeast corner, dedicated to the Supreme God.

②

Puri Saren

🏛️ Jalan Raya Ubud 📞 (0361) 975 057 ⏰ Daily

The grandeur of Puri Saren, Ubud's royal palace, dates from the 1890s, the time of warlord Cokorda Gede Sukawati. The present walls, resplendent gates and stone carvings are largely the work of master artist I Gusti Nyoman Lempad. The traditional buildings are set in a charming garden.

The *puri* (local royal family) still lives here. It remains influential in Ubud's religious and cultural life and spends lavishly on local ceremonies. Nightly traditional dance performances take place at the palace at 7:30pm.

③

Lempad House

🏛️ Jalan Raya Ubud 📞 (0361) 975 618 ⏰ Daily

This is the family home of I Gusti Nyoman Lempad (1862–1978), perhaps Bali's most celebrated artist. Some sculptures by Lempad are on display in the beautiful Balinese garden and a small collection of his line drawings and paintings can be seen inside the house. The Neka Art Museum (*p98*) holds a larger collection of his work.

Lempad was also an architect and builder in the traditional Balinese style, and the handsome north and east

 INSIDER TIP
Tourist Information

The Tourist Information Centre on Jalan Rayan Ubud provides excellent information about guided tours, transport, dance performances and other cultural events in Ubud. It also advises on dress etiquette when visiting temples or traditional religious ceremonies.

pavilions of the house were designed by him. He was the architect of many of the palaces and temples throughout Ubud. As a painter, his line drawings, which drew inspiration from local folklore, were very influential in the Balinese art scene.

Ubud Market

📍 Jalan Raya Ubud, opposite Puri Saren Palace
🕐 Daily

Ubud's huge, busy market is where the Balinese do their shopping early each morning before much of the fresh produce is whisked away to make room for more tourist-oriented handicrafts. Spices, fruits, vegetables, hardware, textiles and woven baskets are all available amid the chaos of the heaped stalls. Everything sold here is grown, crafted, or produced in Bali. If you're more interested in purchasing souvenirs or artwork, visit the market later in the day and you'll find stalls specializing in woodcarvings, wind-chimes, paintings, bags, quilts, sarongs, silk scarves, traditional textiles such as *ikat*, and all manner of handicrafts including lamps, coasters and wooden trays. All of these are handmade in the surrounding craft villages. Bargaining is essential.

Pondok Pekak Library and Learning Center

📍 East side of the football field, Monkey Forest Rd
🕐 9am-5pm Mon-Sat, 1-5pm Sun 🌐 pondok pekaklibrary.com

The library here has more than 30,000 books, including bestsellers, philosophy titles, memoirs and children's books, many in English.

Dedicated to preserving Bali's traditional culture and art practices, the superb, friendly learning centre offers visitors fun classes in traditional Balinese dance, gamelan music, making Balinese offerings, fruit carving, cooking, silver jewellery making, painting, wood-carving, mask-making and other crafts. This is a great place for families, as many of the classes are geared towards children.

↑ Stalls displaying an array of brightly coloured handicrafts at Ubud Market

⑥

Neka Art Museum

📍 Jalan Raya Sanggingan, Campuhan 🕐 9am–5pm Mon–Sat, noon–5pm Sun 📞 (0361) 975 074

Founded in 1976 by art connoisseur Suteja Neka, the museum consists of a series of pavilions presenting an overview of the different historical styles of Balinese painting. This ranges from classical narrative Wayan painting and the Ubud and Batuan styles to contemporary works. The Arie Smit Pavilion is devoted to this Dutch-born artist, while the East-West Annexe showcases other international artists, including Miguel Covarrubias, Rudolf Bonnet, Han Snel and Donald Friend. You can also see black-and-white photographs of Bali during the 1930s and early '40s by Robert Koke, and Bali's largest collections of art by I Gusti Nyoman Lempad.

↑ Stone figure holding a *keris* (traditional dagger), Neka Art Museum

EAT

Murni's Warung

Ubud's first real restaurant, created in 1974 by Ibu Murni, who still owns and runs it, is famous not only for its excellent local food dishes but also for its art displays.

📍 Jalan Raya Campuan, Ubud 🌐 murnis.com

⑦

Blanco Renaissance Museum

📍 Jalan Raya Campuhan, Campuhan Bridge 🕐 9am–5pm daily 🌐 blancomuseum.com

The late Spanish artist Antonio Blanco (1912–99), captivated by Bali, built this palatial house and studio at the top of a steep driveway in Ubud next to Campuhan Bridge in the 1950s. The flamboyant Blanco is best known for his romantic, idealised paintings, collages, illustrated poetry and lithographic artworks, whose main subjects were women. Among his models were his Balinese wife – the celebrated dancer Ni Ronji – and their daughter.

The main gallery is a massive, sumptuous hall with marble floors, huge pillars and a domed roof. The colourful walls are lined with about 300 of Blanco's artworks in lavish and unusual frames displayed in chronological order, as well as some paintings by his son, Mario. The beautiful, cascading gardens house a waterfall, friendly parrots and other birds and offer good views over the river.

Did You Know?

Showing your teeth can be interpreted as a sign of aggression by macaques.

⑧

The Sacred Monkey Forest Sanctuary

📍 Jalan Monkey Forest, Padangtegal 🕐 8:30am–6pm daily 🌐 monkeyforest ubud.com

Ubud's Monkey Forest jungle offers protection to more than 600 long-tailed Balinese macaques, which are fascinating to observe, especially with their young. Follow the paved pathways through the forest and be sure to conceal your camera and other shiny objects, as the mischievous macaques may snatch them and run off in a flash (if this happens, ask the staff for assistance).

There are also three temples here, founded in the 14th century. The largest is the Pura

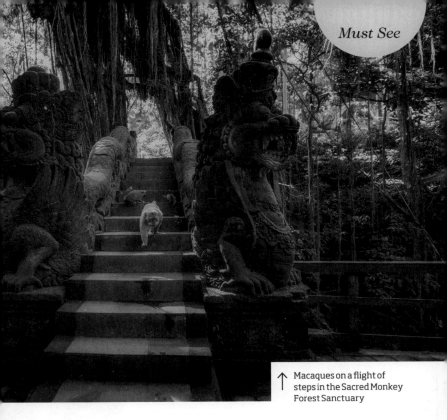

↑ Macaques on a flight of steps in the Sacred Monkey Forest Sanctuary

Dalem Agung (Great Temple of the Dead), with its ornately carved gate located at the highest point of the forest. A long flight of steps and a bridge over a river leads to the Holy Bathing Temple, while the third temple, the Pura Prajapati funeral temple, is situated next to one of two graveyards in the forest. Despite its small size, the forest has around 115 different species of trees.

Jalan Hanoman

Running parallel to Monkey Forest Road, Jalan Hanoman is lined on both sides with small, glass-fronted shops selling homewares, jewellery, clothing and art. Catering to Ubud's thriving community of spiritual seekers, many of the clothing stores sell yoga gear and accessories ranging from intricately designed

Himalayan *cakra* and *mandala* paintings, Tibetan singing bowls, crystals and meditational beads to musical instruments to accompany chanting meditations, aromatic incenses and burning oils. The street is also home to a wide selection of restaurants and small cafés, many of which are vegetarian. Hanoman is the monkey god and his image can be seen at temples along the street.

INFLUENTIAL VISITORS OF THE 1930S

In the 1920s and 1930s, international guests of Ubud's royal family brought attention to Bali. Through their films, books and photographs, these visitors projected to the world an alluring image of Bali. Among the most influential were German painter and musician Walter Spies *(right)*, Dutch painter Rudolf Bonnet and Mexican artist Miguel Covarrubias, who wrote the classic *Island of Bali* (1937). American and English anthropologists Margaret Mead and Gregory Bateson lived in Sayan, just outside Ubud; their neighbours were Canadian composer Colin McPhee and his American wife, ethnographer Jane Belo.

⑩ 🖉 🎨 🍴 🖥 🛍

UBUD MUSEUM PURI LUKISAN

🏠 Jalan Raya Ubud 🕐 9am–6pm daily 🚫 Public hols
🌐 purilukisanmuseum.com

With superb examples of all schools of modern Balinese art, Museum Puri Lukisan ("Palace of Painting") has a large collection of paintings and wood-carvings and is one of the leading art galleries and museums in Bali.

The brainchild of Ubud's prince Cokorda Gede Agung Sukawati and Dutch painter Rudolf Bonnet, the museum was conceived in 1953 out of concern that Bali's finest works of art were disappearing into private collections around the world. Its holdings are mainly 20th-century Balinese painting and wood sculpture, including the colourful paintings of the Batuan School, the highly stylised art of Sanur and the intricately detailed pieces of the Ubud style, with a focus on the 1930s.

LOOKING AT BALINESE PAINTINGS

The density of Balinese painting is extraordinary. Even with little or no background in the arts, the viewer can enter the imaginative world of Balinese culture as represented by both traditional and modern painting. It is a good idea to look at a Balinese work from a distance at first, to see its graphic composition before moving nearer to inspect the details of the content. Close inspection reveals tiny scenes being enacted by the inhabitants of the canvas, a bit like a comic strip.

Dewi Sri (1960), rice goddess with a grain of rice in her hand, by Ketut Djedeng

↑ Main entrance gate to the Museum Puri Lukisan, set in gardens with ponds, and *(inset)* gallery in the museum displaying modern Balinese art

EXPERIENCE MORE

3

Batubulan

🅰E4 🚌 ℹUbud; (0361) 973285

Although Denpasar's urban sprawl is enveloping Batubulan and the main road is lined with shops selling "antique" furniture, this large village is still a centre of traditional stone carving. Craftsmen can be seen in countless workshops sculpting mytho-logical and religious figures or highly imaginative modern forms, apparently oblivious to the heavy traffic passing by.

The village temple, **Pura Puseh** (entry with donation), is a good example of the use of *paras*, Bali's ubiquitous grey stone, which is in fact volcanic tuff, quarried from river gorges. *Paras* is used both for sculpture and as a building material. Its soft texture makes it easy to carve.

Batubulan is also home to several venerable Barong and *keris* dance theatre troupes. During alternate weeks the Pura Puseh hosts a daily performance (starting at 9:30am) by the celebrated Denjalan troupe; in intervening weeks the venue is Batubulan's *bale banjar*, or community pavilion. Other troupes may also take part. These daytime performances began in the 1930s, so that visitors might take photographs. However, this exorcistic drama still has ritual significance.

Pura Puseh
🏠 Main Road, Batubulan
🕐 Daily

4

Bali Reptile Park

🅰E3 🏠Jalan Serma Cok Ngurah Gambir, Singapadu (next to Bali Bird Park) 🕐9am–5pm daily 🚫Nyepi 🌐balireptilepark.id

The Bali Reptile Park (Rimba Reptil) can be visited together with the Bali Bird Park *(p94)* next door, on the same entrance ticket. Although somewhat smaller than the Bird Park, the Reptile Park is also set in lush, botanically interesting gardens. The landscaping concept is that of an ancient archaeological site, excavated and restored to its former glory. Among the native Indonesian species are Komodo dragons, four species of crocodiles, and possibly the largest known python in captivity. Venomous snakes from around the world include a king cobra, a Malayan pit viper and a death adder.

5

Celuk

🅰E3 🚌 ℹUbud; (0361) 973285

The village of Celuk is devoted almost entirely to gold- and silversmithing. Much of the jewellery sold in Bali originates here. The workers belong to the caste clan of Pande Mas, traditionally practitioners of various metal crafts. Grand jewellery shops line the main road; smaller ones selling cheaper goods occupy the narrow side streets. Several

Batubulan's Pura Puseh, a venue for traditional Barong and *keris* dance performances →

BALINESE SILVER JEWELLERY

Using the most basic of tools, Balinese silversmiths handcraft intricate designs from sterling silver, enhanced by a technique called granulation, where small pellets and tiny coiled silver wires are heated until soft enough to adhere to the piece to form a pattern or decorative feature. These miniature works of art are then set with precious and semi-precious gemstones. Styles are distinctive and constantly replicated.

studios make traditional and modern jewellery designs to order, as well as *keris* daggers and religious items. Be aware that at larger outlets, prices may include a fat commission passed on to tour guides.

Batuan

△ E3 ➌ 𝑖 Ubud; (0361) 973 285

Batuan, an ancient settlement predominantly home to Brahmans (considered to be the most noble caste in Bali's social structure), is celebrated for its artistic excellence not only in the field of dance but also in painting and architecture. Painters' studios abound in the village. The Batuan school of painting is known for its dense graphics, restricted colour palette and astute observation of human life.

The Pura Puseh, the magnificent village temple, welcomes visitors. Extensively renovated, its opulent shrines and carvings are proof that Bali's traditional building arts are thriving. *Gambuh* performances are held at the temple at 7pm on the 1st and 15th of each month, a rare opportunity to see this ancient court dance.

Sukawati

△ E3 ➌ 𝑖 Ubud; (0361) 973 285

Sukawati is worth visiting primarily as a handicrafts centre. Opposite the farmers' market on the east side of the main road is the Pasar Seni ("Art Market"): a complex of two-storey buildings packed with craft stalls. Behind it is a market selling woodcarvings, open until 7pm daily.

To the people of Bali, Sukawati is important as the ancestral seat of many of the region's *puri* (noble houses), and as a centre of the sacred shadow puppet theatre, *wayang kulit*. In the early 1700s an offshoot of the royal house of Klungkung was established here, but its palace is now greatly reduced and the temples are not generally open to visitors.

Blahbatuh

△ E3 ➌ 𝑖 Ubud; (0361) 973 285

The village of Blahbatuh is marked by a huge stone statue of a baby, erected in the early 1990s. It is said by some to be the village giant Kebo Iwo as an infant; others whisper that the women of a nearby village urged their husbands to build the statue to placate a demon who they believed had been claiming the lives of their children.

Vihara Amurva Bhumi Blahbatuh, a Chinese temple *(klenteng)* with Buddhist and Hindu elements which has expanded in grand style, is an increasingly popular centre of worship for Chinese Buddhists from throughout South Bali.

Outside the village on the Bedulu road is the large workshop and showroom of the **Sidha Karya Gong Foundry**, established by the renowned gongsmith I Made Gabeleran. A full array of traditional musical instruments and dance costumes is on sale.

At Kutri, 3 km (2 miles) north of Blahbatuh, is a hill at the base of which is the Pura Bukit Dharma Kutri temple complex. On the hilltop, from which there are good views, is a shrine that houses a partly effaced, but still fine, relief carving of the goddess Durga killing a bull. It is thought to be based on an 11th-century Balinese queen.

Sidha Karya Gong Foundry
🏠 Jalan Raya Getas-Buruan, Blahbatuh ☎ (0361) 942 798

> To the people of Bali, Sukawati is important as the ancestral seat of many of the region's *puri* (noble houses), and as a centre of the sacred shadow puppet theatre, *wayang kulit*.

Baskets of fresh local produce at the central market in Gianyar

Sanghyang dance, which could only be staged in the temple. Then, in the early 1930s, artists from Bona developed a fire dance using the story of Ramayana as a substitute for the Sanghyang dance so that it could be performed in public.

⑨ Gianyar

E3 From Ubud
🅘 Ubud; (0361) 973 285

This town is a centre of administration rather than of the tourist industry. The people of Bali shop here for farm produce, household appliances and paraphernalia for ceremonies; there is also a large night market. This is a good place to buy jewellery and hand-woven and hand-dyed textiles, many of them made locally. However, it is particularly popular for its food stalls, which cook a range of delicious dishes; the *babi guling* (roast pig) is famous.

STAY

Komune Resort
A remote black-sand beach is home to this 66-room retreat and beach club, with organic restaurant, spa and pool. The theme here is surfing, yoga and wellness.

E3 Jalan Pantai Keramas, Medahan, Blahbatuh
🅦 komuneresorts.com

On the north side of the town square is the impressive Puri Gianyar. Although the palace is closed to visitors, its grand outer walls and gates give a sense of the power of the former kingdoms. After damage by an earthquake in 1917, the *puri* was restored as a replica of the original 17th-century construction.

⑩ Bona

E3 Between Blahbatuh and Gianyar

Southwest of Gianyar, several villages increasingly make their livelihood by crafting products from native plant materials. Although these are sold for export and in shops around Bali, tourists can buy them for much better prices at source. The village of Bona specializes in making bamboo furniture. However, the attractive items hand-woven by the artisans here from dried lontar fan-palm leaves are perhaps more practicable purchases for the visitor. The variety is enormous and the quality is good; in addition to baskets, hats, sandals, wallets and fans there are also dolls, flowers and even Christmas trees.

Bona is also the place where the dramatic modern Kecak dance was born. Kecak was originally the music that accompanied the sacred

⑪ Bedulu

E3 From Ubud
🅘 Ubud; (0361) 973 285

This large, quiet village was at the centre of the Pejeng kingdom of the 10–13th centuries. The monumental relief carvings on a large rock wall at the **Yeh Pulu** spring, south of the village, are thought to date from the mid-14th-century Majapahit takeover (*p54*). The carvings – about 25 m (80 ft) long with an average height of 2 m (6 ft) – are thought to be the work of a single artist. Myth attributes the work to the legendary 14th-century giant Kebo Iwo. The stories can be "read" from left to right. Among them are shadow puppet characters, Hindu gods and ordinary people. Striking battle scenes show humans fighting demonic beasts.

The large Pura Pengastulan temple has grand gates built in the Art Deco style made fashionable by the artist I Gusti Nyoman Lempad, who was born in Bedulu. Lempad's style may be seen also in the inner gate at the nearby **Pura Samuan Tiga** (entry with donation). Its name derives from a legend: in the 11th century, a meeting (*samuan*) is said to have been held here among the gods of three (*tiga*) warring religious sects after they had defeated the demon king Mayadanawa.

Even when empty, this temple has a great, quiet strength, but it bursts into life during the annual festival on the full moon of the twelfth month in a brilliant 11-day celebration. Don't miss the Perang Sampian warrior ceremony at lunchtime: a graceful procession by white-clad women followed by rowdy mock-fighting among crowds of young men brandishing elaborate palm-leaf whisks.

Yeh Pulu
⊗ ⧖ 7am–6pm daily

Pura Samuan Tiga
⧖ Daily

Mas

🄰 E3 🚌 From Ubud
🄻 Ubud; (0361) 973 285

The village of Mas is most famous not for teak furniture, as the number of roadside shops selling it might suggest, but for fine wood sculpture and *topeng* masks used in theatre performances. The Brahmans of Mas have been master-carvers for many generations, producing sculpture for the art market since the 1930s. Among the best-established studio-galleries are Siadja & Son, the Njana Tilem Gallery and Adil Artshop. Tantra Gallery and I B Anom (for masks) are also well known. Brahmans come to Mas from all over Bali during every Galungan festival *(p52)* to honour their ancestor, the Hindu priest Dang Hyang Nirartha (also known as Dwijendra) at the Pura Taman Pule. The large old tree in this temple is regarded as holy. According to local belief, a gold flower once grew from it. On the evening of the festivities there is usually a ritual performance of *wayang wong* (where characters wear masks and move like puppets).

↑ Carved water buffalo skull, an example of Mas craftsmanship

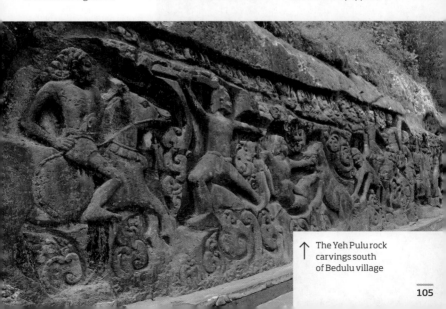

↑ The Yeh Pulu rock carvings south of Bedulu village

Goa Gajah

△E3 ⊠From Ubud
ℹ Ubud; (0361) 973 285
◷ Daily

The Goa Gajah ("Elephant Cave") is thought to date from the 11th century. Steps lead down to a temple and other monuments, about 15 m (50 ft) below road level. The large springs, excavated in 1954, were probably intended for bathing and as a source of holy water. The cave itself, with a large face exuberantly carved in the surrounding rock, is a small, rather airless, T-shaped chamber in which are niches containing Shivite and Buddhist statues.

Outside the cave is a shrine to the Buddhist child-protector Hariti, depicted as the Balinese Men Brayut, a poor woman with too many children. In a ravine a little to the south is a spring and more shrines.

Pejeng

△E3 ⊠From Ubud & Gianyar ℹ Ubud; (0361) 973 285

Pejeng, a village on the road from Bedulu to Tampaksiring, lies at the heart of the ancient Pejeng-Bedulu kingdom, and there are many interesting relics from that time to be seen. The **Museum Purbakala** *(Archaeological Museum; entry with donation)* displays fascinating prehistoric objects in bronze, stone and ceramics, including several turtle-shaped stone sarcophagi.

Nearby are three temples known for their sacred stone sculptures. Just across the road from the museum, Pura Arjuna Metapa (Arjuna Meditating Temple) is a small pavilion standing alone in the rice fields, sheltering a cluster of stone sculptures that were probably once part of a spring temple. In accordance with the *wayang* tradition that recounts tales from the *Mahabharata*, Arjuna is attended by a stone-relief servant character.

About 100 m (110 yards) north is Pura Kebo Edan (Crazy Giant Temple), whose demonic statuary suggests that this was a cult-temple of Bhairava Buddhism. The chief figure is a masked 3.6 m- (12 ft-) high giant, dancing on a corpse. At the beautifully proportioned Pura Pusering Jagat (Navel of the World Temple), numerous pavilions house similar Tantric stone figures. The Pejeng Vessel, a cylindrical stone urn carved with cosmological figures, is kept in a shrine in the south-eastern corner of the temple.

About 2 km (1 mile) north of Pejeng, Pura Penataran Sasih houses the Pejeng Moon (*sasih* means moon), a bronze drum 186 cm (74 inches) long, of unknown age. Considered sacred, it is kept in a tall pavilion. Temple guides sometimes allow visitors to stand on the base of an adjacent shrine; from here, you can glimpse the drum's fine geometric patterning. The design is associated with the Dong-son culture of southern China and northern Vietnam of around 1500 BC.

Museum Purbakala
⌂ Pejeng 📞 (0361) 942 347
◷ 8am-4pm Mon-Fri

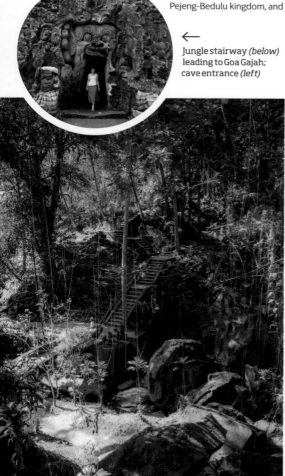

← Jungle stairway *(below)* leading to Goa Gajah; cave entrance *(left)*

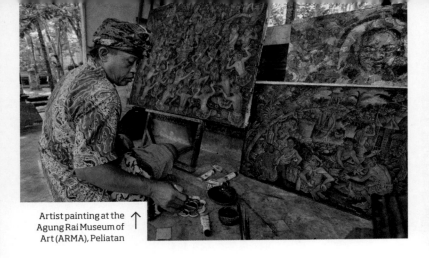

Artist painting at the Agung Rai Museum of Art (ARMA), Peliatan

> **The Agung Rai Museum of Art offers classes in painting and gamelan and many other cultural courses.**

 15

Peliatan

🅰 E3 🏛 🚌 From Ubud
ℹ Ubud; (0361) 973 285

The village of Peliatan, once the seat of an offshoot of the royalty of Sukawati, has long been renowned for its artistic traditions. Today, Peliatan's gamelan and dance troupes travel abroad as cultural ambassadors, as well as performing locally.

Peliatan is also a centre of painting and woodcarving. Many artists' studios can be found along its main street and back lanes. The collector Agung Rai established the successful Agung Rai Gallery and the impressive **Agung Rai Museum of Art** (ARMA). Its collections include classical Kamasan paintings on tree bark, works by Batuan artists from the 1930s, pieces by Javanese and Balinese masters and paintings by Walter Spies, Lempad, Bonnet and Le

Mayeur. There are also contemporary Balinese and Indonesian works. The museum offers classes in painting and gamelan and many other cultural courses.

Also of note is the **Rudana Museum**, which houses traditional paintings by Balinese artists, as well as some modern works.

The northern part of Peliatan, known as Andong, has some interesting craft shops.

Agung Rai Museum of Art

 📍 Jalan Pengosekan
🕐 9am–6pm daily
🌐 armabali.com

Rudana Museum

📍 Jalan Cok Rai Pudak 44
📞 (0361) 975 779 🕐 9am–5pm daily 🌐 museum rudana.org

16

Ayung River Gorge

🅰 E3 🚌 From Ubud
ℹ Ubud; (0361) 973 285

Between Kedewatan and Sayan, the east bank of the spectacularly beautiful Ayung River Gorge is discreetly populated with luxury hotels and private houses. Several companies offer white-water rafting from points on both sides of the river.

In the village of Penestanan, just east of the gorge, there are studios producing painted batik and beadwork. This is also the centre of the Young Artists movement, which emerged in the 1960s. Influenced by Dutch artist Arie Smit, who lived in Penestanan, these artists produced paintings in very bright, vivid colours.

WOODCARVING IN BALI

The surprising abundance of Balinese woodcarving reflects not only an intense decorative tradition but also the fact that Bali's wilderness is forest. Trees have a ritual anniversary and must be given offerings before being felled. Traditional woodcarving is of two main sorts: ritual objects such as effigies and masks; and ornamental carving, especially of architectural elements. The liberalizing art movement of the 1930s encouraged woodcarvers to sculpt freely for a foreign market. The main centres of woodcarving today include Peliatan and several other villages in Gianyar regency, including Tegallalang (p108) and Mas (p105).

Emerald-green bathing pool at the Tegenungan Waterfall near Kemenuh

17
Kemenuh
⚠E3 🚗9 km (6 miles) south of Ubud

The village of Kemenuh has a long-standing woodcarving tradition. Workshops and galleries selling wooden sculptures of animals and mythological figures can be found throughout the village.

Two trekking trails lead from the village through the spectacular scenery of the Petani River Valley. The main attraction here is the 20 m (65 ft) high **Tegenungan Waterfall**, which is framed by dense foliage and accessed down a stairway of 172 steps. At the vast pebbly base of the falls, you can enjoy a dip in the plunge pool, and there are several cafés nearby.

Tegenungan Waterfall
⊕ 🏠 Jalan Raya Tegenungan, Kemenuh, Sukawati ⏰Dawn–dusk

18
Petulu
⚠E3 🚌From Ubud & Pujung 🚉Ubud; (0361) 973 285

In the late afternoon every day, a remarkable, natural phenomenon occurs in the tiny village of Petulu as thousands of white *kokokan* (egrets and pond herons) fly in to roost for the night. The huge flocks of birds arrive in a steady throng, filling the sky, wheeling and finally landing in the tall palms and old fig trees, where they squabble over prime perches. Village tradition dictates that the herons, which are considered sacred, may not be disturbed while they roost.

The V-formations of birds against the background of the sunset form an unforgettable sight. Visitors are welcome to watch them from the upper floor of the village community building. Another good viewing spot is the road from the Junungan direction through the rice fields.

It is not known why the birds suddenly settled in Petulu in 1965. According to local legend, they are the souls of the estimated 500,000 Balinese people killed during the anti-Communist massacres of 1965–6.

19
Tegallalang
⚠E3 🚌From Ubud 🚉Ubud; (0361) 973 285

The captivating village of Tegallalang, once the seat of a kingdom, is interesting as a centre of the woodcarving industry. Workshops and simple wholesale outlets line the road for some 5 km (3 miles), selling a variety of wooden handicrafts at very low prices. There are several small cafés along the main road that overlook the truly spectacular, lush rice

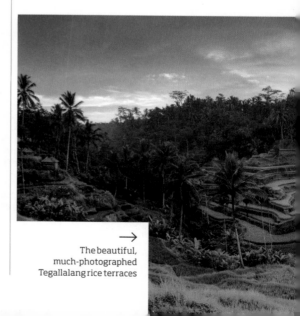

→ The beautiful, much-photographed Tegallalang rice terraces

terraces sculpted into the side of the river gorge north of Tegallalang.

Not far from here, Kebon is a pretty village reached by a steep side road 3 km (2 miles) north of Tegallalang. At the junction with the main road is the excellent Kampung Cafe (0361 901 201), a restaurant with several suites of accommodation. Kenderan, also on a back road, is a former microkingdom with several small puri (houses of the nobility).

The village of Manuaba, about 4 km (2 miles) north of Kenderan, is notable for its Brahman temple **Pura Griya Sakti**, with its refurbished wantilan performance pavilion. A visit to see the huge intertwined trees behind the inner courtyard requires permission of the temple attendant.

There is an interesting holy spring, Telaga Waja, in Kapitu, 1 km (half a mile) south of Kenderan. Access is by way of a 200-m (220-yard) footpath and a long, steep flight of steps. There are traces of meditation niches which suggest that Telaga Waja was once a Buddhist retreat, possibly over 1,000 years ago.

Pura Griya Sakti

 Manuaba Daily

20
Sebatu

E2 From Ubud
Ubud; (0361) 973 285

Sebatu village, part of a larger area of the same name, is highly regarded among the Balinese not only for its painted wood sculpture but also for its dance, music and classical dance costumes. Easily explored on foot, the village is laid out on a grid of three north–south streets, with the temples and bale banjar (community pavilion) at the northern end. The westernmost street is lined with studios making woodcarvings that are offered for sale to visitors.

In a little valley on the western outskirts of Sebatu itself is the lovely spring temple **Pura Gunung Kawi**, not to be confused with the royal monuments of the same name near Tampaksiring (p110). The bathing pools, fed via carved stone waterspouts, are worth seeing (but should not be photographed if they are in use), as is the carp-filled spring pool in the northwest corner. In the centre of the pool is a handsome shrine. There are several interesting sculptures among the small, colourfully painted pavilions in the central courtyard.

Pura Gunung Kawi

 Daily

PICTURE PERFECT
Lose the Crowds

So beautiful are the rice terraces of Tegallalang that the road above is firmly on the tourist photo-op circuit. For some different, more immersive viewpoints, ask one of the locals for a guided visit into the fields. A small fee is expected.

Taro

🅐E2 *i* Ubud; (0361) 973 285

Taro is said to be one of the very earliest settlements in Bali. At the village centre is the large Pura Gunung Raung temple. Looking over its walls it is possible to admire the long *bale agung* pavilion, and a glowering three-tier *meru* pagoda. The latter represents the East Javanese mountain Gunung Raung, from where the legendary sage Rsi Markandya and his followers set out in the 8th century on a mission to Bali that ended here.

Taro is the source of Bali's albino cattle, valued for their importance in large rituals. Formerly they were sacrificed; today they are merely lent out for the ceremony and then returned. The herd wanders freely in the forest south of the village.

Also in Taro is *Lembah Bidadari* (Angel's Valley), where a trail leads through the jungle to a hidden natural spring, near the village of Sangaji. It gets busy in the afternoon, so come in the morning to have this pretty spot all to yourself.

Tampaksiring

🅐E3 From Bedulu & Gianyar *i* Ubud; (0361) 973 285

Tampaksiring is most famously the site of the 10th-century water temple of **Tirta Empul**.

Here, clear freshwater springs, said possess magical curative powers, bubble up within the temple and gush out through spouts into an elaborately carved bathing pool. Locals flock to this holy place in search of blessings and cleansing rituals.

Nearby is **Gunung Kawi**, approached via a steep descent flanked by rice fields. This is the site of ten ancient royal shrines dedicated to 11th-century Balinese royalty, carved out of the rock face of the Pakerisan River Gorge.

Tampaksiring is also home to the serene, picturesque **Pura Mengening** water temple, where a holy spring emanates from under a banyan tree.

North of Tirta Empul is the Presidential Palace, an opulent hilltop retreat built in the 1950s for Indonesia's first president, the half-Balinese Sukarno. It overlooks Tirta Empul and the story goes that the dictator would spy through a telescope on the naked women bathing below. Visitors wishing to enter the palace must apply in writing to the Presidential Office in Tampaksiring, and a formal dress code is applied.

Tirta Empul
◈ 🄰 Jalan Tirta, Manukaya
🕓 7am–6pm daily

Gunung Kawi
◈ 🄰 Banjar Penaka
🕓 7am–6pm daily

Pura Mengening
◈ 🄰 Jalan Tirta, Sareseda
🕓 7am–6pm daily

PRESIDENTIAL PHANTOM

Don't be surprised if you feel a shiver down your spine at the Presidential Palace at Tampaksiring. President Sukarno died in 1970, but local legend has it that his ghost still roams the palace.

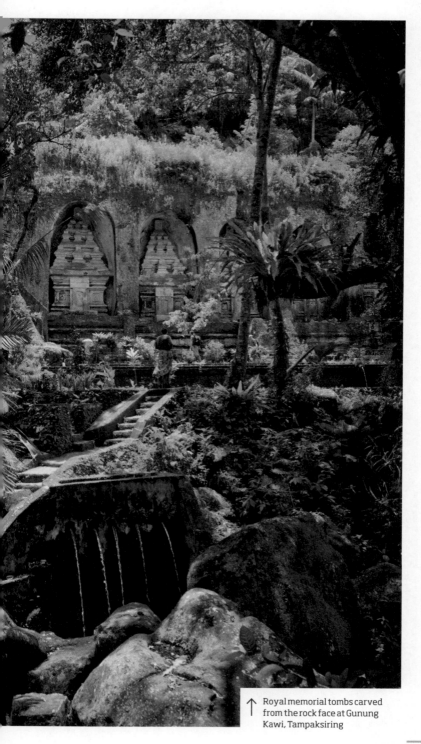

↑ Royal memorial tombs carved from the rock face at Gunung Kawi, Tampaksiring

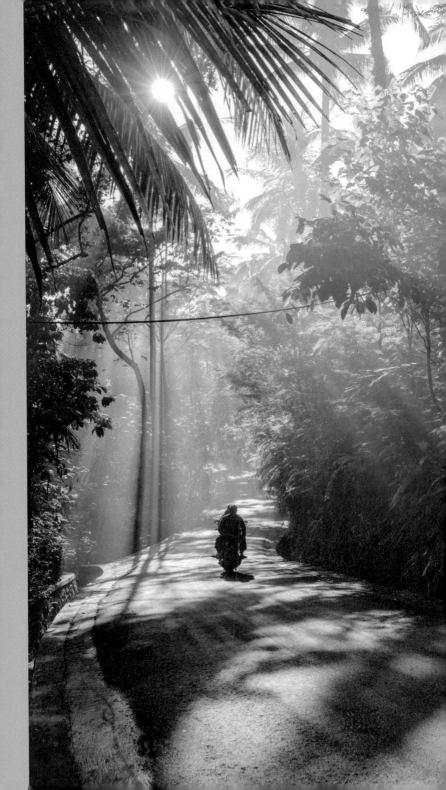

EAST BALI

When the Hindu Majapahit empire fled from Java to Bali in the 14th century, they introduced a new social order and caste system to the island. Some communities resisted it, and their descendants (known as the Bali Aga, meaning "original Balinese"), still live in East Bali's isolated, mountainous areas in culturally distinct villages, such as Tenganan and Trunyan. These Indigenous communities have maintained a rural lifestyle and stayed independent from the rest of the island.

After the decline of the Majapahit, King Dalam Baturenggong consolidated a unified Balinese state in Gelgel, near Klungkung, in 1550. East Bali became the political centre of the island. When Baturenggong's creation broke down in 1651, the region split into the kingdoms of Klungkung, Bangli and Karangasem. One by one these kingdoms came under Dutch control in the late 19th and early 20th century. Karangasem, whose influence extended over the western side of Lombok, fell to the Dutch in 1894; Bangli became part of the empire in 1907; and Klungkung's royal house came to an end in 1908, when the king and members of his court committed *puputan* (mass ritual suicide), rather than submit to Dutch colonial control.

Late in the 20th century, East Bali was hit by a wave of natural disasters, including the eruption of Gunung Agung in 1963 and an earthquake in 1976. In many places, great lava flows transformed the landscape and, due to this geology, as well as the region's Indigenous communities, East Bali feels and looks very different from the rest of the island.

EAST BALI

Must Sees
1 Besakih Temple Complex
2 Gunung Batur
3 Pura Ulun Danu Batur
4 Klungkung
5 Tenganan Bali Aga Village

Experience More
6 Tirtagangga Palace
7 Bangli
8 Iseh
9 Sidemen
10 Gelgel

11 Goa Lawah Bat Cave Temple
12 Candi Dasa
13 Ujung
14 Padang Bai
15 Tulamben
16 Amlapura
17 Pura Lempuyang
18 Amed
19 Gunung Agung
20 Pura Tegeh Koripan
21 Kintamani
22 Bayung Gede Village

Baturinggit
Kubu
Rubaya
Dukuh
15 TULAMBEN
Batudawa

*B a l i
S e a*

18 AMED
Culik   Lipah
Datah
Kahangkahang
Tista   *Bukit
                Biadan*
Abang   Ngis
              Tista
Ababi Bias   **17** PURA
              LEMPUYANG
6 TIRTAGANGGA
    PALACE   Bukit
Budakling   Kebon
Bebandem   Seraya
    AMLAPURA
Bungaya   **16**
                  Yehburg
          13 UJUNG
TENGANAN   Jasri
5 BALI AGA
    VILLAGE
Nyuhtebel Perasi
        Bugbug Pasir Putih
12 CANDI DASA

*L o m b o k
S t r a i t*

EAST BALI

0 kilometres   5
0 miles   5

N

Lombok

1

BESAKIH TEMPLE COMPLEX

F2 **Besakih, Rendang, Karangasem Regency** **Dawn to dusk daily**
Jalan Diponoegoro, Amlapura; (0363) 21 196

For more than 1,000 years, Pura Besakih, Bali's most sacred, impressive, powerful and austere place of worship, has rested at an altitude of 900 metres (3,000 ft) on Mount Agung's southwestern slope. Known as the "Mother Temple", this sprawling complex comprises 22 temples united through ritual and history into a single sanctuary.

Holy Place of Worship

Overlooking stunning scenery of rice fields, hills, valleys, streams and forests beneath the watchful gaze of the mighty Gunung Agung volcano, Besakih's setting gives it a mystical quality. For the Balinese, visiting the complex is a truly special pilgrimage. Every day, hundreds of devout Hindus can be seen solemnly climbing a giant stairway to pay homage to the gods in an atmosphere thick with the smoke and scent of burning incense.

The many different temples and shrines vary considerably according to their status and function, and although you can visit most of them, many of the inner courtyards are reserved for religious pilgrims and are closed to the public. Most of the temples cluster around Pura Penataran Agung, the largest and most important sanctuary in the complex. The highest temple, Pura Pengubengan, lies amidst beautiful groves within a pine forest.

←

Standing in a gateway in the impressive Besakih Temple Complex

> **THE TRIMURTI**
>
> Meaning "three forms of God" in Sanskrit, the Trimurti is the Hindu trinity. These three principal deities are especially revered in Bali. Pura Besakih is said to be their home. Pura Penataran Agung, with white banners, is dedicated to Shiva, the destroyer, in charge of ignorance; Pura Batu Madeg, with black banners, represents Vishnu, the preserver, in charge of balancing good and evil; and Pura Kiduling Kreteg has red banners and is devoted to Brahma, the creator, in charge of passion.

↑ Looking out over the roofs of the temples of Pura Besakih against a backdrop of hills and forests

Did You Know?

Besakih is Bali's only temple open to all devotees of any caste group.

↑ Worshippers climbing the stairway to the Pura Besakih Temple Complex

Pura Penataran Agung

The Great Temple of State, Pura Penataran Agung is the central, the largest and the most dramatic building in the complex due to its size, position and the great reverence in which it is held. Originating probably as a single, prehistoric shrine, it is the symbolic centre of Besakih, arranged on six levels terraced up the slope, which represent the six layers of the universe, each with their own shrines.

As worshippers climb the giant stairway lined with figures from the Hindu epics – the *Mahabarata* and the *Ramayana* – and pass through the first courtyard, they symbolically sever their connection with the everyday world. In all, there are 57 structures within this temple, about half of which are devoted to various deities, while others have various ceremonial functions, such as providing seating for the priests and the gamelan orchestra. Visitors may not be allowed inside all of the courtyards.

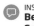
INSIDER TIP
Beware of Scams

In Besakih, you may be approached by a local offering their services as a guide for an over-inflated price. Be polite and playful, yet firm and simply say "*tidak terima kasih*" ("no, thank you"). To save money, bring your own sash and sarong rather than renting one at the temple.

↑ Visitors on the steps leading to Pura Penataran Agung

The tall meru are shrines for deified kings, ancestral spirits and nature gods.

The main courtyard is the principal focus of worship. A padmasana tiga (triple lotus shrine) is dedicated to Brahma, Shiva and Vishnu.

The terraces at the entrance to Pura Penataran Agung are an echo of the stepped pyramids of Indonesian prehistory.

→
Pura Penataran Agung, the spiritual core of the Besakih complex

The grand main entrance stairway leading to the temple

Footpaths connect the temples in the complex.

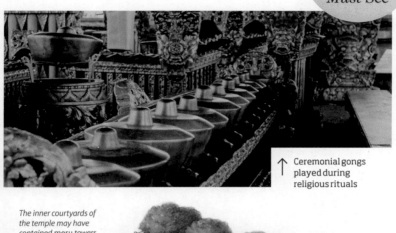

↑ Ceremonial gongs played during religious rituals

The inner courtyards of the temple may have contained meru towers since the 14th century.

Low walls surround the temple; visitors can view the shrines by walking along the footpaths and looking over the walls.

↑ Courtyard inside the temple, and *(inset)* roof of a shrine in front of a *candi bentar* (split gate)

2 (M) (Y) (D) (fl)

GUNUNG BATUR

F2 ⊠ From Penelokan & Kintamani ⊞ From Kedisan *i* Jalan Letulila 9, Bangli, (0366) 91 537; Toya Bungkah Mount Batur Trekking Guides Office, (0366) 52 362

Rising to 1,717 m (5,633 ft), Gunung Batur draws visitors to its summit for the stunning panorama of Bali. Part of its spectacular caldera is filled with Lake Batur, Bali's largest crater lake. Superb views of the volcano can be enjoyed from the nearby village of Penelokan.

Although Gunung Batur is not the largest volcano in Bali, it is the most active. It is surrounded by a massive caldera, which implies that it was once much larger than now, having blown off its top in an eruption. It has erupted on a large scale more than 20 times in the last 200 years. The most devastating occasion was in 1917 when more than 1,000 people died and over 2,000 temples were destroyed. Volcanic activity has made the slopes of Gunung Batur bare and dry, in contrast to the vegetation which covers the slopes of Gunung Abang, on the opposite side of Lake Batur.

The fascinating Batur Geopark Museum (open 8am–5pm daily) at Penelokan near the volcano's crater rim, explains the geology of the volcano through detailed interactive displays and rock samples.

Climbing Gunung Batur

Most visitors use trails that start near Toya Bungkah village. Trekking to the top of Gunung Batur from here typically takes two hours. You can hire a local guide at the Mount Batur Trekking Guides office in the village. The most popular treks are timed for arrival at the summit at dawn to see the sunrise. The air can be quite chilly before daybreak, and warm clothing is highly recommended for night treks. You'll also need a torch. Guides will provide breakfast on the summit for a fee, which can include cooking an egg in the steaming holes at the top of the volcano. The slopes of the volcano can be slippery and dangerous in the rainy season from October to April, and trekking is not recommended during this time.

↑ Sunrise behind
Mount Batur, a truly
spectacular sight

TRUNYAN BALI AGA VILLAGE

One of the culturally isolated Bali Aga villages, Trunyan is perched on the eastern shore of Lake Batur and is most easily accessible by boat from Kedisan. Villagers here practise customs found nowhere else in Bali. These include neolithic funeral rites. Instead of burying or cremating dead bodies, the people place them in pits covered by bamboo canopies to preserve them from being eaten by animals. The forces of nature dissolve the body tissues until only the skeleton remains. Trunyan is also known for the impressive Pura Pancering Jagat temple, inside which is a tall statue of the patron guardian of the village.

1 Swimmers enjoying a geothermally heated hot spring at Toya Bungkah village at the foot of Mount Batur.

2 Lake Batur is the main source of irrigation for much of the agriculture of Central and East Bali.

3 Hikers descend friable terrain in the caldera of Mount Batur volcano.

PURA ULUN DANU BATUR

🄰E2 🄰Jalan Kintamani, Batur Selatan, Kintamani
🄲Daily during daylight hours

This is the second-most-important temple complex in Bali after Besakih *(p116)*. Sitting on the southwestern rim of the Mount Batur caldera, it features nine graceful temples and many shrines.

 INSIDER TIP
Dewi Danu

On the northeastern shore of Lake Batur is a striking yellow statue of Dewi Danu standing on a lotus flower and sea serpent. It can only be accessed by boat – for a small fee, a local boatman from Songan will take visitors across.

Lake Goddess

Ulun Danu literally translates as "head of the lake" and the temple is dedicated to Dewi Danu, the life-sustaining and highly venerated goddess of the lake, who supplies water to the 37 rivers, tributaries, dams and irrigation canals between here and the sea. Lake Batur is the source of dozens of underground springs, which help regulate the flow of water for the farmlands and sacred bathing pools throughout Gianyar and Bangli. Farmers from all over the island come here to pay homage to the goddess who helps bless the island's soil with fertility.

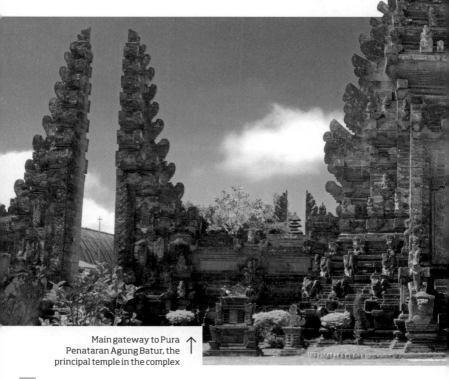

Main gateway to Pura Penataran Agung Batur, the principal temple in the complex ↑

OFFERINGS TO THE LAKE GODDESS

Devotees from all over Bali present elaborate offerings at Pura Ulun Danu Batur. The respect accorded to the goddess of Lake Batur is reinforced by events in the temple's history. At its former location closer to the lake at the foot of the Batur volcano, the temple was miraculously saved from destruction in the volcanic eruption of 1917, when the lava flow stopped just short of its walls. Another eruption, in 1926, prompted the villagers to move it to its present location at the highest and oldest rim of the caldera.

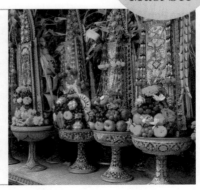

The nine-temple complex, with its impressive tall gateway, contains a maze of more than 200 shrines and pavilions dedicated to the gods and goddesses of water, agriculture, holy springs, arts and crafts. In the northwest corner, a Chinese-style shrine flanked by colourful statues is dedicated to Ida Ratu Ayu Subandar, god of merchants.

→

Tops of gates in Pura Ulun Danu Batur, with Mount Batur in the background

Pura Penataran Agung Batur

With five main courtyards, Pura Penataran Agung Batur is the principal temple in the Pura Ulun Danu Batur complex. The dominant shrines are the pagoda-like *merus*, the most significant of which is the 11-tiered *meru* in the inner courtyard, dedicated to Dewi Danu. There are also three nine-tiered *merus* for the gods of Mount Batur, Mount Agung and Ida Batara Dalem Baturenggong, the 15th-century deified king of Gelgel. The *kulkul* (drum) tower in the outer courtyard houses a wooden split drum that is beaten 45 times each morning to honour the 45 deities worshipped in the temple.

Did You Know?

The main festival here takes place on the 10th full moon in the Balinese calendar (late Mar–early Apr).

→ Layout of the Pura Penataran Agung Batur, with its impressive architectural structures

The third courtyard is the most sacred. Three gateways lead from one courtyard to the next.

The figure of Garuda, a bird from Hindu mythology, is depicted in this stone relief on the courtyard wall.

The great quadrangular central courtyard is the occasional setting for baris gede, *an old ritual dance performed by a regiment of soldiers to protect the deities.*

← A few of the pavilions and *merus* in Pura Penataran Agung Batur

1 Ornate, gold-painted carvings feature on the great timber doors of the main temple gateway.

2 Offerings are carried to the Lake Goddess Dewi Danu by devotees.

3 This beautiful side gate is built in a combination of brickwork and carved stone decoration.

The great timber doors of the main temple gateway are reserved for the use of priests on important occasions.

This tall, slender side gate leads to another temple.

Entrance

The *bale gong* is a pavilion housing the temple's set of gamelan instruments, including a great gong believed to have a magical history.

↑ The Puputan monument, fashioned in dark stone, opposite Taman Gili

4

KLUNGKUNG

⚑F3 ⊞ ℹ Jalan Untung Surapati 3; 0366 21 448

The royal capital of Bali's smallest regency, Klungkung (also known as Semarapura), was the focal point of art and culture during the Gelgel dynasty. In the centre of this bustling trade town is the Taman Gili, the remains of the 18th-century royal palace.

Puputan Monument

⚑ Corner of Jalan Untung Surapati and Jalan Gajah Maja

In 1908, Klungkung was the last kingdom in Bali holding out against the rule of the Dutch invaders. Hopelessly outnumbered, the raja of Klungung, accompanied by 200 members of his family and court, made a desperate sortie out of his palace into the face of the Dutch guns. The raja was armed with a *kris* (dagger) that, according to a prophesy, was supposed to wreak havoc upon the enemy. However, the *kris* failed to fulfill the desired outcome, and the raja was shot by a Dutch bullet. His six wives promptly committed ritual suicide, or *puputan*, each killing herself with her own *kris*, followed by all the other members of the court. The sacrifice is commemorated in the tall Puputan Monument.

Museum Daerah Semarapura

⚑ Corner of Jalan Surapati and Jalan Puputan
☎ (0878) 6246 6055
🕓 8am–5pm daily

To the west of Taman Gili, the small Museum Daerah Semarapura contains old Dutch newspapers recounting the sickening details of the *puputan* massacre in 1908, when 200 members of Klungkung's royal court committed ritual suicide. Interesting exhibits also include the royal litter carriage (*palanquin*), which was bearing the raja when the Dutch opened fire, as well as photos of the raja with his family and the royal court.

Pura Taman Sari

⚑ Jalan Ahmad Jani
🕓 Dawn to dusk daily

The 17th-century Pura Taman Sari temple is a serene place to relax. The name means flower garden and the temple features grassy compounds planted with flowers, and a grey-stone eleven-roofed *meru* surrounded by a waterlily-filled moat.

Klungkung Market

⚑ Jalan Puputan 7 🕓 6am–6pm daily

Hidden in a concrete building to the east of Kerta Gosa, is Klungkung's fabric market, an Aladdin's cave for lovers of traditional textiles. Vendors sell *songket* (a rich brocade) in a wide variety of designs, as well as another of Bali's traditional fabrics, *endek*, for a much lower price than you'd pay elsewhere.

⑤
Kamasan

 1.6 km (1 mile) south of Klungkung

The village of Kamasan is a community of artists. Their work is in the *wayang* style that is found on the Kerta Gosa ceilings of the former royal palace (p128), and only Kamasan artists are allowed to restore the frescoes today.

The rigidly standardised, formal style is stricly flat, one-dimensional and beautifully decorative with rich colours and intricate patterns. Faces are drawn in three-quarters profile, similar to shadow puppets against a screen, and there is no central focal

BALINESE ENDEK

The most common traditional textile in Bali is *endek*, a form of weft *ikat*. A motif is dyed into the threads of a cloth before it is woven using a resist-dye method. Repeated tying and dyeing produces a textile of shimmering multi-hued patterns. In Bali the designs are applied only to the weft threads.

point, yet each painting tells multiple stories. Kamasan art originally had religious themes, and the artists were sent all over Bali to decorate temples and palaces. It was Bali's only form of pictorial representation until the 20th century, when European artists arrived and influenced the Balinese to paint realistic scenes of everyday life.

During Dutch rule, the Kamasan artists lost their royal patronage and their

specific style of art nearly died. Happily, Kamasan underwent a resurgence when the Dutch commissioned the restoration of the Kerta Gosa paintings in the 1920s and 1930s. Since the 1960s, tourists and art shops have been an important source of revenue. You can still buy these cloth paintings, unframed and at very reasonable prices, in various shops in the village. Be generous; these fine traditional artists are masters of their craft.

⑥
Tihingan

 4 km (2.5 miles) west of Klungkung

The centre of production of Balinese gamelan musical instruments, Tihingan village welcomes visitors at craftsmen's workshops. Here you can observe the techniques of the blacksmiths, known as *besalen* and *pande gong*, as they forge, bend and weld metal pieces into gongs and metallophones, and fine-tune each to the perfect pitch. Ritual brass and copper instruments are also crafted, such as the bells used by Balinese priests. As well as making metal gamelan instruments, the master craftsmen also create beautiful pedestals and traditional two-sided drums.

⑦ 🏛 🏚

TAMAN GILI

🏠 Puri Semarapura, corner of Jalan Surapati and Jalan Puputan, Klungkung 🕐 7am–6pm daily 🚫 Public holidays

Dating to the early 18th century, Taman Gili ("moated garden") is what remains of Klungkung's royal palace. The paintings in the Bale Kerta Gosa and Bale Kambang are beautiful examples of the *wayang* style.

Most of of the royal palace was destroyed in 1908 during the Dutch takeover. The main surviving features are two raised, open meeting halls, or *bale*, with intricately painted ceilings. The painted panels arranged in several tiers have undergone restoration and repainting several times in the last hundred years. They follow the traditional *wayang* style, in which the figures resemble shadow puppets (p127). The present structure of the Bale Kambang dates from the 1940s.

This palace was built along traditional lines – Balinese palaces are not huge standalone buildings, but rather a series of courtyards, gilded pavilions, gardens, rice sheds and family temples, linked by a tranquil maze of gateways and alleyways, and enclosed by high walls. Because Balinese kingdoms were defined, not by borders, but by their social and economic hub – the palace was centrally located near the market, which was the focus of artistic and economic activity.

At the apex of the ceiling is a carved lotus flower surrounded by gilded doves, representing the goals of enlightenment and salvation.

There are 267 painted panels arranged in several tiers in the Kerta Gosa.

Entrance

← The peaceful Taman Gili palace, with its pavilions, courtyards, stone statues and bridges

KERTA GOSA CEILING PAINTINGS

The main series shows part of the *Bhima Swarga* narrative, which was incorporated into Balinese tradition from the Indian *Mahabharata* epic. There are also scenes from the *Tantri* stories (a Balinese version of Indian moral fables), and some are based on an astrological calendar, showing earthquakes and eruptions.

Layout of the buildings and gardens forming the Taman Gili royal palace complex

Did You Know?

The main gate is said to have shut on its own after the 1908 *puputan*. Nobody has dared to open it since.

The roof of the Bale Kambang is made of hardwood shingles.

The ceiling paintings in the Bale Kambang depict scenes from Balinese myths, including the story of Sutasoma, a Buddhist saint symbolizing strength without aggression.

The moat surrounding Bale Kambang teems with carp.

The building is surrounded by many carved stone reliefs of mythical creatures.

→

A stone statue of an ancient mythical demon in Taman Gili

⑤ 🛠 🚗 🖥 🏛

TENGANAN BALI AGA VILLAGE

🅰 G3 🏠 3 km (2 miles) west of Candi Dasa 🚌 From Candi Dasa
ℹ Amlapura; (0363) 21 196 🕐 Dawn–dusk

Tenganan village is home to the ancient Bali Aga people, who have lived on the island for centuries. Here, they live according to ancient customs and create beautiful arts and crafts.

Descendants of the original Balinese, the Bali Aga resisted the rule of the Majapahit kings, fiercely safeguarding and maintaining their own culture through the conviction that they are descended from the gods.

One of the island's original pre-Hindu settlements, the village is still a stronghold of Indigenous traditions and the Bali Aga maintain a lifestyle bound by strict *adat* (customary law) practices. A tiny socialist republic, all of the village and surrounding fertile farmland is owned communally. The rice fields are rented out to other farms and profits are evenly divided among the villagers.

The villagers are thus able to devote their time to crafts, including cloth-weaving, calligraphy and basket-weaving. In particular, *geringsing* – double *ikat* textiles – are woven here and worn during the day by the villagers. The ritually significant cloth is believed to protect the wearer from sickness. Cars and motorcycles are forbidden from entering the village.

1 Traditional calligraphy is inscribed onto palm leaf manuscripts.

2 Offerings are presented at traditional ceremonies.

3 Double *ikat* weaving is used to create *geringsing* cloth.

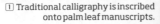

← Street in Tenganan, where the Bali Aga strictly adhere to a traditional way of life of ritual and ceremony

THE LEGEND OF TENGANAN

It is said that in the 14th century, King Bedaulu, the ruler of Bali, lost his favourite horse and offered a reward for its return. The horse was eventually found dead near Tenganan and the villagers asked to be granted land as a reward. In spite of the fact that the horse was dead, the King sent his minister to draw the boundaries of the area to be given to them, instructing the minister to include all of the land where he could smell the dead horse. Accompanied by the village chief, who had cunningly hidden some of the rotting horse meat in his clothes, the minister performed his duties and drew generous boundaries which remain today.

Exploring Tenganan Bali Aga Village

The most striking feature of this neat, walled village is its unique layout. Open-sided community halls and elevated longhouses, including the stately Bale Agung, where the council of elders makes its decisions, have been meticulously positioned in accordance with long-established beliefs. Three parallel avenues run north to south, ascending towards the mountains, each level connected by steep cobbled ramps, while narrow lanes run east to west forming a grid. Single-storey dwellings line both sides of the main street, along with rice barns, shrines, communal pavilions, open kitchens and *bale* administration buildings.

In front of many houses, traditional *ata* vine baskets are laid out in neat rows to dry in the sun. Demonstrations of weaving and other crafts can be seen inside the villagers' houses, which also function as shops and workshops. You can watch calligraphers inscribe elaborate calendars and illustrations on palm leaves with ink brewed from burnt macadamia nuts, weavers create intricate *geringsing* textiles and woodcarvers make masks.

At the northern end of the village, beyond the elementary school, an arched gate opens onto a jungle of towering breadfruit and durian trees, coconut palms and hanging creepers. A few steps up the hill is the beekeeper's house, where visitors are always welcome.

In the village's "temple of origins", the community joins in rituals reflecting a dualistic cosmology based on principles of complementary opposites.

The wantilan *is a large, open pavilion where village members meet for social activities.*

The main streets are partly cobbled and rise in tiers, connected by ramps.

← Bali Aga women carrying harvested coconuts, and *(inset)* rice fields surrounding the village, which are worked by neighbouring farmers

MEKARE-KARE

The *mekare-kare* is an annual theatrical fight in June between the young men of the village using prickly pandanus leaf whips. Each dual is staged to the martial sounds of gamelan *selonding* music and lasts only a few seconds, accompanied by much merriment and laughter. The attacks are warded off with tightly woven *ata* vine shields; there are no winners and no losers because the objective is to draw blood as an offering to the gods. After the battles, the combatants' wounds are treated with alcohol and turmeric, leaving no scars.

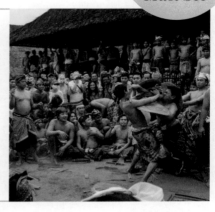

Did You Know?

Tenganan crafts are also sold in specialist shops in Seminyak and Ubud.

Market

The Bale Petemu is the meeting hall of one of three associations of unmarried village men.

The village houses have steps and a courtyard.

← Plan of the well-preserved Tenganan Bali Aga Village

The kitchen of the Bale Agung is where ceremonial meals are cooked.

Entrance

The Bale Agung is the hall for meetings of the village council, composed of all the married couples.

Beautiful terraced rice fields around
Tirtagangga, with Gunung Lempuyang
and Gunung Seraya in the background ↑

A LONG WALK
TENGANAN TO TIRTAGANGGA

Distance 6 km (4 miles) **Walking time** 3 hours
Nearest town Candi Dasa **Transport** *Bemo* to
Candi Dasa, then own transport **Terrain** Hilly

The walk from Tenganan to Tirtagangga reveals
some of the most scenic terrain of Bali's interior, and
many glimpses of traditional Balinese life along the
way. From the higher points there are impressive
views of Bali's mountains; the route also passes
through terraced rice fields and peaceful hillside
villages with beautiful temples.

Ababi

*Bukit
Tiragangga
302 m
(990 ft)*

Tirtagangga
FINISH

*The country road
to Tirtagangga
offers good views
of rice fields with
the sea beyond.*

*Bukit Komala
393 m
(1,289 ft)*

Krotok

*Bukit Dausa
283 m
(928 ft)*

Budakeling

0 kilometres — 1
0 miles — 1

N

Bebandem

*A small café, or hillside
warung, stands on the
slope overlooking the rice
terraces. The trail leads on
to an irrigation dam and a
rice field shrine before
crossing a shallow river.*

*Bukit
Sangyangapi
287 m
(941 ft)*

Kastala

Hillside Warung

Bungaya
Kangin

Gumung
Kaja

*Pura
Puseh*

*The metal-smithing village
of **Budakeling** is north of
the main road before you
arrive at a lava trail.*

*Across the river, the trail
leads to **Kastala village**
near the main road. To cut
short the walk, transport can
be taken from Bebandem.*

*In the village of
Gumung Kaja, baskets
and mats are woven
with the stems of the
ata, a kind of palm tree.*

Bungaya Kauh

*At the **Pura Puseh** temple, a
view to the far east of Bali is
revealed; rice fields
can be seen at various
stages of cultivation.*

*Bukit
Kauh
263 m
(862 ft)*

*From the **Tenganan
village** gate, a stone-paved
path leads to a temple
complex and then to the
edge of the forest.*

Tenganan
START

*Tenganan
Village Gate*

Dauh
Tukad

*Bukit Kangin
315 m
(1,033 ft)*

EAST BALI
*Tenganan to
Tirtagangga*

Locator Map
For more detail see p114

135

EXPERIENCE MORE

Tirtagangga Palace

G3 **Ababi** **(0361) 730374** **Daily**

Tirtagangga (meaning "holy water from the Ganges") is the best surviving example of Bali's royal water palaces. It was built in 1947 by Anak Agung Anglurah Ketut, the last king of Karangasem. The complex consists of a sacred spring, a cold spring-fed pool and several other ponds, all set in lovely gardens. Bathing is permitted in the pools. A small fee is charged at the spring-fed pool, which has simple changing rooms.

Tirtagangga has a cool climate, and is a good base for walks in the area. There are several homestays here.

Bangli

F3 **Jalan Brigjen Ngurah Rai 30; (0366) 91537**

A royal court city from the 14th to the 19th century, Bangli is one of Bali's oldest towns, a small, well-ordered and tidy community set some way up the hills towards Gunung Batur – ideal for a walk in the cool mountain air.

Pura Kehen, a place of worship since the 12th century, steps impressively up a hillside in a series of eight terraces. A huge banyan tree in the first courtyard of the complex conceals an almost invisible *kulkul* – an alarm drum – high in its branches. Fine statuary lines the steps leading to the *padmasana* shrine where there is a multitiered *meru* roof in the inner sanctuary. The shrine is elaborately ornamented and the gold-painted doors of the temple are beautiful. Entry is with a donation.

Pura Penyimpenan ("the temple for keeping things") contains three ancient bronze inscriptions which imply that the area was considered holy long before the present temple complex was built.

Images of heaven and hell, the latter imaginatively grim, cover the walls of **Pura Dalem Pengungekan**, a temple

---

TEXTILES OF EAST BALI

In Bali great importance is attached to textiles and their making. This area is famous for a type of double ikat weave called *geringsing*, produced only in the Bali Aga village of Tenganan *(p130)* and credited by the Balinese with protective spiritual powers. In Sidemen complex, decorative motifs in gold and silver threads are woven into cloth to create a rich brocade textile known as *songket*. This is often worn at religious or social events, and as part of the costume of traditional dancers.

Stepping stones and statuary across the royal ponds at Tirtagangga Palace

great volcanic valleys. The terraced rice fields are lush and green. Iseh itself is a small village with little in the way of tourist facilities. Walter Spies *(p56)* built a house here (now a luxurious rental property), and it was this location that inspired some of his most beautiful paintings.

At Putung, 6 km (4 miles) east of Iseh, there are some great lookout points and a couple of homestays. A further 4 km (2 miles) to the east is the village of Sibetan, the best place to buy *salak*, a small, crisp, tart-tasting fruit with a scaly exterior that looks rather like snakeskin.

⑨
Sidemen

🅰F3 🚌From Bangli and Klungkung 🏛Amlapura; (0363) 21 196

Sidemen is set in some of the most beautiful countryside in East Bali. The views from the slopes of Gunung Agung stretch out like a green patchwork with an impressive mountain backdrop. The town is a retreat from the hustle and bustle elsewhere, and

GREAT VIEW
House Beautiful

The house built by artist Walter Spies at Iseh, now a hotel *(www.villaiseh. com)*, has a breathtaking view of the Sidemen Valley and Gunung Agung, one that has been enjoyed by famous guests such as Mick Jagger and David Bowie.

there are some good homestays overlooking rice fields. In Sidemen you can visit workshops making *songket*. This work is historically the preserve of higher castes, and still implies high social status.

⑩
Gelgel

🅰F3 🚌From Klungkung 🏛Klungkung; (0366) 21 448

The royal court of the Majapahit rulers of Bali *(p54)* was established in Gelgel in the 14th century by Dewa Ketut Ngulesir, son of Bali's first Majapahit king. A reminder of the former kingdom is Gelgel's ancient royal temple of Pura Dasar, with its large outer courtyard, and several tall *meru* towers.

The Pura Penataran is one of several temples along the village's broad streets.

dedicated to the dead, and inside are shrines to Brahma, Shiva and Vishnu.

Pura Kehen
🅰Jalan Sri Wijaya 🕐Daily

Pura Penyimpenan
🅰Jalan Sri Wijaya 🕐Daily
🔒For ceremonies

Pura Dalem Pengungekan
🅰Jalan Merdeka 🕐Daily
🔒For ceremonies

⑧
Iseh

🅰F3 🚌From Bangli and Klungkung 🏛Amlapura; (0363) 21 196

The area around Iseh is remarkable for glorious landscapes. Some of the best can be seen on the road eastward from Bangli via Muncan and Duda, which carves its way east through

The magnificent Gunung Agung, viewed from across the Sidemen Valley

Goa Lawah Bat Cave Temple

⒒F3 🚌 **ℹ️Klungkung;**
(0363) 21 448 🕐Daily

Thought to be more than 1,000 years old, Goa Lawah is important to temple rituals pertaining to the afterlife. The main feature of the temple is a cave inhabited by tens of thousands of fruit bats. Local legend has it that the cave stretches 30 km (19 miles) back into the mountain, as far as Besakih (p116), and is the home of a giant dragon-like snake called Basuki who feasts on bats.

There are some good restaurants outside the cave that have fine views over the ocean towards Nusa Penida and Lombok. However, it is also renowned for hawkers.

Kusamba, 4 km (3 miles) southwest of Goa Lawah, is a busy little fishing village with a black-sand beach. *Jukung* (outrigger fishing craft) line the shore, and are available for chartered day trips to nearby islands. Be aware that the sea can be quite choppy. Salt production pans can be seen here.

Candi Dasa

⒓G3 🚌 **ℹ️Jalan Candi Dasa;**
(0363) 21 002

The fishing village of Candi Dasa is an ideal base for diving, snorkelling, trekking and exploring Bali's peaceful east coast. This beautiful area in the royal Balinese regency of Karangasem has a rich heritage. Here, life goes on as it has for generations. It is a quieter place than other built-up tourist areas in Bali, but still has a full range of accomodation options, as well as spas and restaurants.

The name Candi Dasa was originally applied just to two small temples, one dedicated to Siwa, and the other, on a sacred palm-fringed lagoon beside the beach, to Hariti, goddess of fertility. This is a place of worship for childless couples; the name Candi Dasa is said to be derived from the Balinese "Cilidasa", which means "ten children".

In the Blue Lagoon bay, the water is clear and warm, with abundant marine life amid a coral reef, making it ideal for snorkelling and diving. The hiking around Candi Dasa is also superb. From Bukit Asah near the village of Bugbug,

STAY

Jasri Bay Hideaway
This seafront boutique retreat near Candi Dasa offers five rustic-chic, wooden houses plus a pool and a restaurant serving home-grown organic produce.

⒓G3 📍**Jalan Pura Mastima, Jasri**
🌐**jasribay.com**

Rp Rp Rp

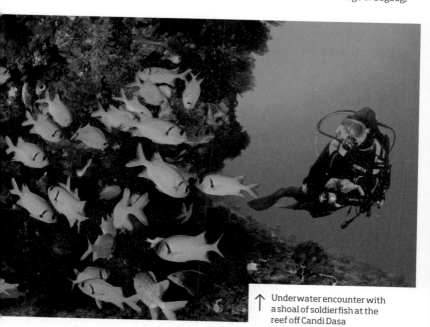

↑ Underwater encounter with a shoal of soldier fish at the reef off Candi Dasa

a 30-minute walk brings you to a hilltop outlook with a beautiful panorama of the sea, the coastline and neighbouring islands. From here, it is just another 10 minutes to Pasir Putih (known as Virgin Beach), a gorgeous, 500-m (550-yard) stretch of sand fringed with coconut palms. Grass-roofed *warungs* offer cold drinks and fresh fish. Visitors can rent sunbeds and umbrellas, and enjoy beach massages.

Ujung

G3 From Amlapura
Amlapura; (0363) 21 196

Ujung, meaning "at the end", is an appropriate name given the remote location of this fishing village. The Puri Taman Ujung is a water palace built in 1919 by the last raja of Karangasem, Anak Agung Anglurah Ketut. The buildings were all but destroyed in the 1976 earthquake but have been restored to their former grandeur.

The narrow road winding east from Ujung around the eastern tip of Bali is very scenic, with spectacular views of the ocean and Gunung Seraya. Before taking this road, it is advisable to check its condition with the locals.

Padang Bai

F3 To Nusa Lembongan, Nusa Penida & Lembar, Lombok
Amlapura; (0363) 21 196

This beach resort makes a good base for exploration and is also the main port for ferries to Lombok, so the traffic from Denpasar is quite heavy. In the village there are numerous restaurants, hotels, guesthouses, bars, tour guides and dive shops.

Within walking distance, to the west of Padang Bai, is Biastugal, an unspoiled white-sand bay where sun-worshippers gather. A little further along the coast it is possible to rent outriggers for diving and snorkelling. At the eastern end of the bay, a 20-minute walk away, there are several temples. They include Pura Silayukti, associated with Mpu Kuturan, who introduced the three-temple system to Balinese villages in the 11th century.

↑ Bridge leading to the main temple building at Puri Taman Ujung

Tulamben

G2 From Amlapura & Singaraja
Amlapura; (0363) 21 196

Tulamben is a nondescript little village, but it is of interest as the location of the wreck of the American cargo ship *Liberty*, 120 m (396 ft) long and torpedoed during World War II. It lies 40 m (44 yards) offshore and, at its deepest point, some 60 m (198 ft) down. The wreck is now covered in coral and inhabited by fish. The water provides great diving and snorkelling. Day trips off Tulamben can be arranged with dive operators. Boats can be rented locally.

> The name Candi Dasa was originally applied just to two small temples, one dedicated to Siwa, and the other, on a sacred palm-fringed lagoon beside the beach, to Hariti, goddess of fertility.

European decorative influence at the royal palace at Amlapura ↑

16

Amlapura

 G3 ◉ ℹ Jalan Diponegoro; (0363) 21196

The small but busy trading town of Amlapura is a district capital with an active market serving the area. The town was given its present name after reconstruction in the aftermath of the 1963 eruption of Gunung Agung. It is still often referred to by its former name, Karangasem.

Karangasem became an important power in the late 17th century. The royal families of Karangasem had strong political links with the nearby island of Lombok. **Puri Agung**, a royal palace of the kings of Karangasem, was built at the turn of the 20th century. It was the birthplace of the last king.

Did You Know?

David Bowie and Tin Machine released a song about Amlapura in 1991.

The palace compound is no longer inhabited, descendants of the royal family preferring to live in the palaces of Puri Gede and Puri Kertasurahe across the road (unlike Puri Agung, these are not open to the public). Architecturally, Puri Agung is an eclectic mix of European and Balinese styles. It has a particularly impressive entrance gateway.

The main attraction is the Maskerdam Building ("Amsterdam" as pronounced by the locals), so-called as a tribute to the Dutch following their takeover of Lombok in 1894, when Karangasem placed itself under Dutch rule. Behind its carved doors are pieces of furniture donated by Queen Wilhelmina of the Dutch royal family. Another building is known as the Bale London, as some of its furniture bears the British royal family's coat of arms.

Just south of Amlapuri, in the beach resort of Jasri, is a hidden gem: the small artisanal **Sorga Chocolate Factory**. Visitors can observe the entire chocolate-making process, from the harvesting of the cacao fruits to the finished, and beautifully wrapped, organic chocolate bars and truffles. A tasting session is a must; chocolate-making workshops are also on offer.

Puri Agung

 ⌂ Jalan Sultan Agung ◷ Daily

Sorga Chocolate Factory

◉ ⌂ Jalan Pura Mastima, Jasri ◷ 8am-5pm Mon-Sat, 8am-noon & 2-5pm Sun ⓦ sorgachocolate.com

---

17 🖵

Pura Lempuyang

 G2 ⌂ Drive through the villages of Tista, Abang and Ngis Tista ◉ ◷ 7am-5pm daily ℹ Amlapura; (0363) 21196

A visit to Pura Lempuyang is well worth a full day trip, especially when there is a temple ceremony taking place. Getting there is part of the attraction – the road from Tirtagangga runs northeast along a picturesque valley, carving its way through rice

→

The view through the split gate at Pura Agung Lempuyang Tara Penah fields. Pura Lempuyang is a complex of seven temples, the most spectacular of which is Pura Agung Lempuyang Tara Penah. Here, a dazzling-white, towering split gate perfectly frames Gunung Agung. The temple guardians – three pairs of colossal sea serpents – border a trio of staircases with Balinese doors at the top.

About 1 km (0.5 miles) further on, another temple, Pura Pasar Agung Lempuyang, marks a stairway of 1,700 steps, with strategic resting places along the way. It winds through the monkey-inhabited forest up to the directional temple of Lempuyang Luhur, 768 m (2,500 ft) above sea level to the southeast of Gunung Agung. It's not large – there is just a single courtyard – but it is one of Bali's oldest and most highly regarded temples, important because of its location. This has probably been a sacred site since pre-Hindu times, and the intense spiritual energy of this place is almost tangible. There's a story that in the 1960s, before electricity reached Bali, a space satellite reported the observation of a blue beam emanating from Earth; the precise location was plotted and the source was confirmed as Pura Lempuyang Luhur.

Amed

🅰G2 🚌 🛈 Amlapura; (0363) 21 196

Amed is the collective name given to a series of fishing villages that lie along about 10 km (6 miles) of the island's easternmost shore, via a rollercoaster of a road that coils around steep headlands, sheltered coves and scalloped, grey-sand beaches cluttered with traditional *jukung* fishing boats. With fabulous sunset views of Gunung Agung and brilliant sunrises over Lombok, this laid-back area has some of the best coral reefs and dive sites on the island. It is also the start-point for trekking up the slopes of Gunung Seraya.

Dive resorts, hotels and restaurants are plentiful here. Salt production is carried out on the beach, and local fishers take visitors out in their traditional boats.

The sleepy market village of Seraya itself is perched on the cliffs above the rocky coast. It is believed to be the first village to weave the sacred black-and-white chequered *poleng* cloth that you see all over Bali, draped around trees and statues and worn at ceremonies. The weaving industry has been revived here. The villagers grow natural dye plants such as morinda and indigo around the edges of their fields and you can watch the women weaving traditional Seraya textiles.

EAT

Warung Enak
This charming restaurant serves traditional Balinese dishes.

🅰G2 🏠Purwakerti, Amed 📞(0819) 1567 9019

Sails Restaurant
On a hillside with sea views, Sails offers Mediterranean cuisine.

🅰G2 🏠Bunutan, Amed 📞(0363) 22 006

Aquaterrace
Delicious Indonesian and Pan-Asian dishes are served at this clifftop restaurant.

🅰G2 🏠Selang Bunutan, Amed 🌐aquaterrace-amed.com

⑲ Gunung Agung

🅰 F2

Mighty Gunung Agung, the highest point on Bali, is a 3,014-m (9,888-ft) active volcano, and the dominant feature of East Bali. The Balinese believe it to be an earthly replica of Mount Meru, central axis of the universe, and as such it has a profound significance in their lives. Communities orientate their houses, temples and even beds in relation to this sacred place, where the spirits of ancestors are thought to dwell.

The barren, lava-scoured eastern flanks of Gunung Agung bear witness to its most devastating eruption in recent history, in 1963. According to local belief, this was violent retribution for the mistiming of a lengthy religious ceremony that must be performed all over Bali every hundred years to placate the demon gods of danger.

However, the volcano is now active again and therefore, for reasons of safety, it is currently forbidden to climb Gunung Agung. But even on the lower slopes, visitors should be aware that they are in the vicinity of a holy place: observe the rules for temple dress (*p199*) and refrain from disrespectful behaviour.

> ### THE POWER OF GUNUNG AGUNG
>
> The Gunung Agung volcano is capable of cataclysmic eruptions accompanied by the phenomenon of pyroclastic flow, in which a cloud of deadly burning gases powers down the mountainside ahead of the lava stream. The latest period of eruption activity, both seismic and volcanic, began in 2017, and prompted the evacuation of 122,500 people from their homes. An EDA (Estimated Danger Zone) of 6 km (4 miles) around the volcano has been in place since this time. In May 2019, southern Bali was covered in ash after a 4.5-minute eruption.

⑳ Pura Tegeh Koripan

🅰 E1 🚌 From Kintamani
🕒 During ceremonies
ℹ Penelokan; (0366) 51 370

Also known as Pura Sukawana or Pura Penulisan, Pura Tegeh Koripan is one of the oldest temples in Bali, dating from the 11th century or earlier. Set at more than 1,500 m (4,950 ft) on the side of Gunung Penulisan, it is certainly one of the highest. It is little visited by tourists and, therefore, has a peaceful atmosphere.

The site is in fact a complex of five temples. Its pyramidal structure, set on eleven levels of terraces along the slope, suggests that it dates from the pre-Hindu-Buddhist era, and is associated with the megalithic culture of Bali.

The main temple, Pura Panarajon, dedicated to the god of the mountains, is over 300 steps up, at the highest position in the complex. Inside, there are some stone inscriptions and statues thought to date to the 10th century.

From the slopes of Gunung Penulisan there are good views: on clear days you can see as far as Java to the east, and the Bali Sea to the north.

21

Kintamani

🅰E2 🚌 🛈Penelokan;
(0366) 51 370

One of the most popular destinations for visitors in Bali is Kintamani, notable above all for its view of a volcano within a caldera. The air here is fresh and the view from Kintamani into the caldera of Gunung Batur *(p120)* is perhaps the most famous on the island, as the tourist buses testify.

Kintamani is one of three small villages, along with Penelokan and Batur, set high on Batur's caldera rim. It is hard to distinguish where one ends and the next begins, as they have merged together to form a ribbon of development catering for the many visitors and tour buses that come here. Arriving early in the day helps avoid the crowds and provides the best photo opportunities as afternoons can be cloudy.

However, people do not come to look at the village of Kintamani itself – they come to stand in awe of the view. It is worth stopping here just to get a real sense of the scale of the landscape from a high vantage point; here it

is easy to see the relative positions of Gunung Batur, the Bali Aga village of Trunyan *(p121)* down on the shore of Lake Batur, and Gunung Abang on the eastern side of the lake facing Gunung Batur.

Lake Batur lies within a much more ancient caldera here, and is fed by hot springs; bathing facilities are offered at Toya Bungkah. There are many places to eat along most of the 10 km (6 miles) of the main road along the crater rim; there is also a volcano museum and a market selling fresh local produce.

22

Bayung Gede Village

🅰E2 🅰8 km (5 miles)
southwest of Kintamani

The small village of Bayung Gede is a place where time has stood still. Believed to be the first village of the Bali Mula, the earliest inhabitants of the island, it dates back to pre-Hindu times and still maintains the traditions established by its founders. The village has a quiet pace and an almost complete lack of vehicular traffic. The north–south running streets, with their houses sheltered behind

←
Smoke and steam issuing from Gunung Agung during an active period

↑ Floating pier with a bar and pleasure boats at Lake Batur, Kintamani

mud-brick walls, are home to more than 2,000 residents, and a protective wall of living bamboo surrounds the whole community. Roofs are made of interwoven bamboo tiles; when new roofs are needed, families and friends come together in *gotong royong* (shared work) to raise a new roof. Bayung Gede is the real deal, not a stage-managed tourist site. Nevertheless, visitors are welcomed here.

EAT

Bali Asli
This restaurant/ cooking school in the foothills of Gunung Agung offers glorious views. It serves classic Balinese food created from home-grown produce and cooked in a traditional Balinese-style kitchen on wood-fired, mud-brick stoves.

🅰G2 🅰Jalan Raya Gelumpang, Gelumpang
🌐baliasli.com.au

Ⓡ Ⓡ Ⓡ

NORTH AND WEST BALI

This area corresponds to the regencies of Tabanan, Jembrana and Buleleng, of which the administrative capitals are Tabanan, Negara and Singaraja respectively. The population is increasingly Muslim as you move west; the older Muslim settlements were established by Bugis sailors in the 17th century who came to Bali to escape the Dutch invasion of Sulawesi in 1667.

The history of this part of Bali has been influenced as much by the sea as by the traditions of the courts: both Singaraja and Negara have the flavour of Javanese coastal trading towns than of the Balinese centres of aristocratic power. North Bali is more heavily marked by the Dutch colonial presence than the rest of the island, which was colonized later. Following their brutal takeover of Buleleng in 1849, the Dutch set up a Residentie (prefecture) in Singaraja in 1855. Singaraja shows evidence of its Dutch past in its old offices and mansions and the airy, shady atmosphere of the town. It was from Singaraja and the surrounding area that the Dutch launched their final campaigns against the southern Balinese kingdoms of Badung, Tabanan and Klungkung between 1906 and 1908. The European press criticized the violence of these battles, which they branded massacres. In an effort to clean up their international image, the Dutch implemented many measures to preserve Balinese culture, but they also introduced the transmigration program by which they moved people from densely populated areas of Indonesia to less populous ones in the country. This practice continued even after Indonesia declared independence in 1949 and many north Balinese were forced from the area after the eruption of Mount Agung in 1963. The migration slowed the development of tourism in North and West Bali, and today the regions are sought out by visitors wanting to escape the crowds.

NORTH AND WEST BALI

Must Sees

1. Taman Nasional Bali Barat
2. Singaraja
3. Pura Meduwe Karang
4. Pura Taman Ayun

Experience More

5. Pura Tanah Lot
6. Kapal
7. Pejaten
8. Krambitan
9. Tabanan
10. Bali Butterfly Park
11. Marga
12. Blayu
13. Sangeh
14. Sangeh Monkey Forest
15. Yeh Panas
16. Gunung Batukaru
17. Pura Gangga
18. Perancak
19. Negara
20. Medewi Beach
21. Gilimanuk
22. Makam Jayaprana
23. Menjangan Island
24. Pemuteran
25. Pantai Gondol
26. Banjar
27. Munduk
28. Pupuan
29. Lake Tamblingan
30. Lake Buyan
31. Lake Bratan and Bedugul
32. Lovina
33. Jagaraga
34. Gitgit
35. Tejakula

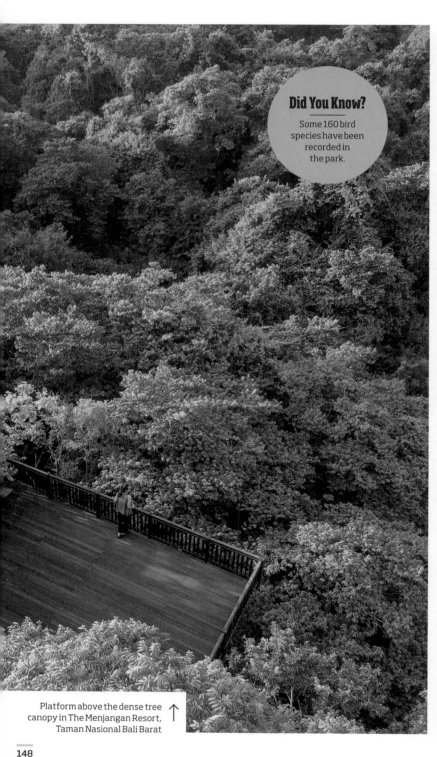

Platform above the dense tree canopy in The Menjangan Resort, Taman Nasional Bali Barat

1 🚶 ♿

TAMAN NASIONAL BALI BARAT

B2 ℹ Park Headquarters: Jalan Raya Gilimanuk, Cekik; (0365) 610 60

The far west of Bali is occupied by the spectacular Taman Nasional Bali Barat (West Bali National Park), administered by the Indonesian Forestry Service. This wildlife reserve, established by the Dutch in 1941, is bordered by a large area of protected land. The reserve aims to safeguard Bali's remaining wilderness and provides sanctuary for some threatened species.

Here you can hike through thick rainforests, explore open, dry savannas and coastal mangrove swamps, and snorkel around Menjangan Island. The park is home to more than 200 plant species and over 300 different species of animals and birds, most particularly the rare and endangered Bali starling. Other protected fauna include the scaly anteater, the black giant squirrel, the Malayan porcupine and the marbled cat. Permits are required for anyone who wants to enter the park (apply at the Park Headquarters) and visitors must be accompanied by an official guide. Only travel on foot is allowed.

THE BALI STARLING

The Bali starling (*Leucopsar rothschildi*) is the only surviving bird endemic to Bali and one of the world's most endangered bird species. Since 2005 efforts have been made to raise their numbers. The conservation project at West Bali National Park aims to save the species, by breeding the birds in captivity before releasing them to the wild.

↑ The sea around Menjangan Island, rich in fish and coral

Highlights

Nature Walk

▽ A short trek with a guide from the park headquarters passes by rivers and through rainforest. Along the route are several forest shrines.

Grasslands

Fertile grasslands stretch out towards the sea near the quiet beach of Pantai Gondol. A fishery research project is located here.

Sambar Deer

▲ The forested mountain slopes are the habitat of Sambar deer, which roam freely in the park.

Balinese Sapi

These local cattle, descended from the now rare wild banteng, have been domesticated for heavy work in the rice fields.

Mangroves

▲ Mangrove roots protect the coast from erosion; the wetlands are home to fish, mudskippers and crabs.

↑ Pasar Anyar market stalls selling fresh produce and flowers

2

SINGARAJA

🚍 Terminal on Jalan Surapati, Jalan Ahmad Yani & at Sangket ℹ️ Jalan Veteran 2; (0361) 25 141

North Bali's main commercial centre, Singaraja was the administrative capital of Bali in colonial times and is Bali's second largest city after Denpasar. With its charming waterfront and Dutch colonial buildings, this historic royal city is a pleasant place to stroll.

 ①

Chinese Temple

📍 Jalan Erlanga 65
📞 (0368) 263 32

With its classical red roof titles, decorated with tablets in gold calligraphy, this temple indicates the strong presence and influence of the Chinese trading community in this part of Singaraja.

 ② 🛍️

Pasar Anyar Markets

📍 Jalan Dipenogoro and Jalan Gajah Mada
🕐 24 hours daily

There are two markets in Singaraja. The market at Jalan Dipenogoro has a wealth of busy stalls selling fresh fruit, vegetables, fish, meat, flowers and utensils, while the smaller one on Jalan Gajah Mada sells all manner of handicrafts and souvenirs, and becomes particularly lively after sundown when the temperature cools.

 ③

Pura Jagat Natha

📍 Jalan Pramuka

Singaraja's main temple is a large complex of buildings covered in fine stone carvings. Evening *gamelan* rehearsals take place in one of the court-yards. Entry is with a donation.

④

Puri Singaraja Royal Palace

📍 Jalan Mayor Metra
📞 (0362) 229 74
🕐 4–6pm daily

Often also referred to as the Puri Agung or Puri Gede, this royal palace, originally built in

↑ Traditional Balinese carved timber veranda, in Puri Singaraja palace

Did You Know?

Singaraja is one of the few places in Bali where Dutch, Chinese and Islamic influences can be seen.

the early 17th century, was the main residence of the rulers of the kingdom of Buleleng. It was destroyed by the colonial Dutch invaders and then rebuilt in the early 19th century. The palace is a fascinating network of interlocking open courtyards and traditional Balinese architecture of single-storey houses, shrines and temples. It is open for guided tours.

⑤
Puri Sinar Nadiputra

🏠 Jalan Veteran, next to Gedong Kertya
🕒 Mon–Thu & Sat

Housed in a former palace is the Puri Sinar Nadiputra weaving factory, where you can observe the textile-making process and buy the products. Silk and cotton *ikat* cloth is sold in the adjacent shop.

⑥
Independence Monument

🏠 Jalan Pelabuhan Buleleng

At the old harbour and waterfront is the striking Independence Monument showing the freedom fighter Yudha Mandala Tama pointing out to sea. He was killed by gunfire from a Dutch warship when he replaced the Dutch flag with the Indonesian flag early in the struggle for independence. The harbour and its pier is one of the most picturesque parts of town.

⑦
Gedong Kertya

🏠 Jalan Veteran 20 & 22
📞 (0362) 22 645 🕒 8am–4pm Mon–Thu (from 9am Fri–Sun)

Founded by the Dutch in 1928, Gedong Kertya is a museum displaying a vast collection of old Balinese *lontar* books and manuscripts, the only *lontar* museum in the world. The books cover subjects such as history, literature, mythology and religion. There are also some even older works in the form of inscribed copper plates called *prasati*, which feature traditional stories.

⑧
Nagasephaha

🏠 8 km (5 miles) south of Singaraja

The village of Nagasepaha is famous for its tradition of glass painting. Its initiator was a local puppet master,

LONTAR

An iconic example of Bali's heritage, *lontar* books are made from fan-shaped *rontal* palm leaves. The leaves are dried, soaked in water, cleaned, steamed, dried again and then flattened, dyed and cut into strips. These are inscribed with words and illustrations using a very sharp stylus and are then coated with a black stain, which is wiped off, making the marks legible.

Jero Dalang Diah, who used to carve the characters for his stories out of buffalo or cow leather before painting them. In 1950, he was inspired by a Japanese glass painting and began to paint on glass, using images from Balinese *wayang* stories. Today, his descendants and several neighbours in the village practise this artform and sell their glass paintings.

3 🕒

PURA MEDUWE KARANG

🅰 E1 📍 Jalan Raya Air Sanih, Kubutambahan ☎ (0361) 235 600 🚌 From Singaraja 🕐 8am–5pm daily

The large "temple of the landowner", built in the late 19th century and dedicated to agricultural spirits, is notable for its statuary and carved panels.

Did You Know?

Meduwe Karang is the god of protection of agricultural land.

Considered one of Bali's principle temples due to its size, Pura Meduwe Karang has a flowery style of decoration characteristic of the north of the island. There are successive split gates and a set of two symmetrical *gedong,* or pavilions. The highest point is the towering, elaborately decorated Betara Luhur Ing Angkasa shrine. The most famous and unusual sculpted panel is on the base of the main plinth in the inner enclosure. It is a highly stylised depiciton of a man riding a bicycle with a lotus flower serving as the back wheel.

The long pavilion at the side of the forecourt is used for gatherings during festival celebrations.

→
Plan of the layout of Pura Meduwe Karang

The grand parade of 34 stone figures lined up on the entrance terrace are all characters from the Indian Ramayana epic.

Terraces at different levels are linked by steps.

←
Stone sculptures of figures from the ancient Indian *Ramayana* poem

At each level of the temple the ascent to the main shrine passes through a candi bentar (split gate) decorated with relief carvings.

A westerner on a bicycle, with a lotus flower serving as the back wheel, is depicted on the side of the main shrine.

The impressive Betara Luhur Ing Angkasa main shrine honours the "Lord possessing the ground". Offerings are also made at the shrine to the sun-god Surya and to Mother Earth for fertility of the agricultural land.

Sculptures illustrating subjects from Balinese legend decorate the walls around the central courtyard.

Reliefs adorning the courtyard walls show people and scenes from everyday life.

Elaborately carved paduraksa (stone posts)

Ornate columns in place of walls distinguish this temple from others in Bali.

The walls of the courtyard are reinforced at intervals by pillars topped with carved decorations.

1. The temple entrance has three rows of *Ramayana* statues.

2. A stone figure of the temple's guardian angel at the entrance.

3. This carving of a man riding a bicycle is thought to be of Dutch artist W O J Nieuwenkamp, who is said to have brought the first bicycle to Bali in 1904.

PURA TAMAN AYUN

🅰️ D3 🏠 Mengwi ☎ (0361) 756 176
🚌 From Denpasar 🕐 9am–6:15pm daily
🚫 Some sections closed to public except during festivals

The Taman Ayun ("Vast Garden") temple, in its moated setting, symbolizes the Hindu world set in the cosmic sea. It features beautiful traditional architecture set in expansive gardens with lotus and fish ponds.

Located on an axis connecting the mountains with the sea, Pura Taman Ayun is thought to ensure the harmonious circulation of water from the mountains of Bali to the rice fields, then to the sea, and back to the mountains. The *meru* towers represent the mountains, residence of the gods.

Originally established around 1634 by the then-ruler of the Mengwi kingdom, the temple was restored in 1937. In it are the ancestral shrines of the former ruling Mengwi family and their dependants, as well as shrines dedicated to particular mountains, such as Gunung Batur, Gunung Agung and Gunung Batukaru, to the sea and to agricultural deities.

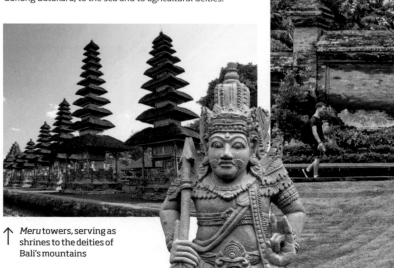

↑ *Meru* towers, serving as shrines to the deities of Bali's mountains

→ Traditional stone carved statue on the wooden pavilion in Pura Taman Ayun

Did You Know?

The brick walls delineating the main temple areas are built the traditional way, without mortar.

↑ Kori Agung, the main gate to Pura Taman Ayun, and *(inset)* detail of a statue of Sai, a guardian figure on the lintel of the gate

EXPERIENCE MORE

5

Pura Tanah Lot

🅐 D4 🏠 Tanah Lot
🚌 From Denpasar & Kediri
ℹ️ Tabanan; (0361) 880
361 🕐 6am–7pm daily

One of Bali's most heavily promoted landmarks, Pura Tanah Lot is a temple set dramatically on a small island about 100 m (110 yards) off the coast. It can get very crowded, and it is best to arrive well before sunset, when there are not too many visitors around. As the sun goes down, the shrines make a magnificent silhouette against a glowing horizon – a memorable sight despite the throngs of visitors at this time. The many handicraft, souvenir and refreshment stalls at Tanah Lot are a major source of income for the region's women and children.

The islet – a promontory until the beginning of the 20th century – is accessible on foot at low tide, but only Balinese Hindus may go inside the temple. It is being eroded by the onslaught of the sea. The cliffs around the island have been carefully reinforced with concrete, and tripods have been sunk into the sea to act as breakwaters.

As its name suggests, the temple is situated at the meeting point of land *(tanah)* and sea *(lot)*. The part that faces the sea is dedicated to the Balinese goddess of the sea, Betara Tengah Segara, while the landward side is thought to be the seat of the gods from Gunung Batukaru *(p160)*. The temple is associated with the saint Dang Hyang Nirartha. He is said to have advised its construction in order to protect Bali against scourges and epidemics; these destructive forces were thought to originate from the sea.

Along the nearby coast, numerous temples and shrines have been built to protect Tanah Lot. They include Pura Pekendungan, Pura Jero Kandang, Pura Galuh and Pura Batu Bolong.

The last of these, a short distance north of Pura Tanah Lot and rarely visited by tourists, is at the end of a rocky promontory that leaps seaward to form a natural bridge over the waters of the Indian Ocean.

6

Kapal

🅐 E3 🚌 From Kediri and
Denpasar ℹ️ Tabanan;
(0361) 811 602

The most conspicuous feature of Kapal is hundreds of shops selling ready-made temple shrines and somewhat kitsch cement statues. There is also some attractive earthenware.

In a quiet street leading off the main road is **Pura Sada**, the temple of origin of the royal house of Mengwi. A donation is expected to enter. Damaged during an earthquake in 1917, it was rebuilt in the 1960s by a team of Indonesian archaeologists,

The temple at Tanah Lot, where land and sea meet, and *(inset)* one of its guardian statues

rows of mini-shrines in the temple yard are said to commemorate the crew of a ship that sank while transporting to Bali the sacred effigy of a Majapahit king.

Pura Sada
🏠 Banjar Pemebetan, near Banjar Celuk, Kapal ⏰ Daily

---

❼ Pejaten
📍D3 🚌 From Denpasar & Tanah Lot ℹ️ Tabanan; (0361) 811 602

The village of Pejaten is home to a considerable cottage industry that produces terracotta roof tiles, earthenware, pots with coloured glazes, and other decorative objects often attractively naive in character. It is a good place to browse and bargain.

About 3 km (2 miles) northeast of Pejaten is the village of Kediri, where an ornate white statue marks its centre. Kediri is important locally for its cattle market and colourful

based on the 17th-century original. The most interesting part is the 11-tier stone *meru* built in the style of a Javanese *candi*. Such towers are known as *prasada*, and are very rare in Bali. This example is a reminder of the kings' claimed descent from the Majapahit *(p54)*. The tall, 16-m- (53-ft-) high phallic form emphasizes its dedication to the Hindu god Shiva. Affixed to the sides of the tower are images of the eight lords of the compass directions. Vishnu and Brahma with Shiva, the deities of the Hindu Trimurti (triad), are portrayed on the eastern side. On the lower base of the tower are represented the seven seers of the Hindu-Balinese cosmos. The *candi bentar* (split gate) is decorated with sets of Boma (guardian spirit) heads on the front and back; these are split like the gate itself. The closely packed

fabrics. The road from here south to Tanah Lot crosses enchanting rural landscapes.

---

❽ Krambitan

📍D3 🚌 From Tabanan ℹ️ Tabanan; (0361) 811 602

The small town of Krambitan was an old agrarian kingdom until the turn of the 20th century. It still has a village-like atmosphere and some old architecture. Krambitan is an important repository of Balinese classical culture.

There are two very interesting 17th-century royal palaces, Puri Anyar and Puri Agung Wisata. It's possible, for a donation, to look around the lovely buildings and pavilions. Occasionally, "royal parties" of Balinese dance take place, complete with torches and *tektekan*, a form of gamelan music in which *cenceng* (cymbals) are augmented by bamboo sticks or wooden cowbells.

Klating Beach, on the coast 6 km (4 miles) south of Krambitan, is an unspoiled black-sand beach with some simple *losmen* (guesthouses) available nearby.

TAKE A PEEK AT PALACE LIFE

When the royal estates of Puri Anyar were confiscated under the 1961 law of Land Reform, the enterprising family turned their hands to hospitality, hosting fabulous banquets for visiting politicians, ambassadors and celebrities. If the gates are open, you're welcome to have a look around the vast, antique-filled compound; if you're very lucky, the prince himself will give you a tour.

Tabanan

🗺 D3 🚌 **From Denpasar** 📍 **Jalan Gunung Agung; (0361) 811 602**

This is a bustling commercial town. The interesting, if somewhat rundown **Museum Subak** has mock-ups of the *subak* irrigation systems of Bali, whereby associations are formed by owners of land irrigated by a common water source. Traditional farming implements are also displayed. Entry is with a donation.

Surabrata, also called Balian Beach, 30 km (19 miles) west of Tabanan, is charming. It has a fishing village set by a cliff, and a small river called "Sacred River" – a name intended to appeal to visitors. The surfing is good and basic accommodation is available.

Museum Subak

🏛 Jalan Gatot Subroto, Sanggulan ⏰ 8am–12:30pm Fri (to 4:30pm Sat–Thu) 🚫 Public holidays 🌐 museum-subak.business.site

Bali Butterfly Park

🗺 D3 🏛 **Jalan Batukau, Sandan Wanasari** 📞 **(0831) 1935 6846** ⏰ **9am–4pm Mon–Fri (to 5pm Sat & Sun)**

Located in the Tabanan regency, Bali Butterfly Park (Taman Kupu-Kupu Bali) is Indonesia's largest butterfly enclosure – an educational conservation area for the preservation of butterflies and insects. A visit to the park is an opportunity to encounter rare and endemic species of butterflies, which are best seen on dry days in the early mornings when they are at their most active. The park promotes the study, breeding and preservation of the 15 known species of butterfly that thrive in Indonesia's tropics, as well as various other insects and arachnids, in extensive and informative displays. Visitors have the opportunity to see the many stages of metamorphosis, from egg, larvae and pupae to cocoon and newly emerged butterflies drying their wings. Colourful and protected specimens include the common birdwing (*Troides helena*), the Bali peacock (*Papilio peranthus*) and the paradise birdwing (*Ornithoptera paradisea*).

Marga

🗺 E3 🚌 **From Denpasar & Mengwi** 📍 **Tabanan; (0361) 811 602**

The village of Marga was the site of a battle between the Dutch and the Balinese guerrillas in 1946. On the western side of the village is the Margarana Monument. Besides the graves of the 95 guerrillas who died in the battle of Marga, the garden contains monuments to 1,372 key figures of the War of Independence in the 1940s. The graves do not resemble Christian, Muslim or even Hindu graves: they are small, *meru*-shaped structures reminiscent of the ancient temples from the Javanese empire of Majapahit (*p54*).

The central monument, not to be mistaken for a Balinese *meru* shrine, is designed to symbolize the day of the proclamation of independence, 17 August 1945. The four steps and five small pillars at its foot represent the year (45); the eight tiers of its roof give the month (August); and the height of 17 m (56 ft) gives the day (17). A statue of Gusti Ngurah Rai (*p57*) completes the scene.

Blayu

🗺 E3 🚌 **From Denpasar & Kediri** 📍 **Tabanan; (0361) 811 602**

Blayu, like nearby Mambal, is a scenic village on a road lined with beautiful *kori* house gates typical of the area. Near the village is the monkey forest of Alas Kedaton. In the temple, **Pura Alas Kedaton**, is an ancient statue of Ganesha, the Hindu god of knowledge.

Pura Alas Kedaton

🎟 🕙 ⏰ Daily

BATTLE OF MARGA

In 1946, after Japan surrendered at the end of World War II, the Dutch strove to re-establish their colonial authority in Bali. Local nationalists led a guerrilla war against them. On 20 November 1946, 95 Balinese fighters commanded by Gusti Ngurah Rai were trapped by Dutch troops near Marga. Surrounded on the ground and strafed from the air, they fought to the last, in a modern repeat of the ritual *puputan* (mass suicide). The Margarana Monument pays tribute to their sacrifice.

The temple in the Sangeh Monkey Forest, and *(inset)* a long-tailed macaque ↑

 Sangeh

⚐ E3   ⊟ From Denpasar
ℹ Tabanan; (0361) 811 602

The village of Sangeh is home to an inspiring community rural tourism project. Local guides lead visitors on a gentle trek through a forest of fruit trees, past small farms, to Tirta Taman Mumbul, where huge trees shade an emerald-green lake, inhabited by giant koi fish. An enchanting water temple, Pura Ulun Mumbul, appears to float upon the lake, while a lofty banyan tree shelters a small statue of an elderly water-bearer. Legend has it that the old woman stopped for a rest at this spot, took pity on the dry land and watered the shrivelled-up plants; miraculously, the water continued to pour from her small jar to form the lake t hat we see today.

On the opposite side of the road is Pancoran Solas, a holy spring, which is channelled into a shallow bathing pool through eleven waterspouts guarded by statues of eleven Hindu gods. The Balinese come here to receive a ritual blessing while bathing in the purifying waters. Close by is Pondok Jaka, an old Balinese compound and farm, featuring traditional grass-roofed houses with bamboo walls, rendered with a mixture of mud and rice husks.

 Sangeh Monkey Forest

⚐ E3   ⊟ From Denpasar
◷ 8am–4pm daily
ℹ Tabanan; (0361) 811 602

Monkeys are found in many gorges and mountains in Bali, and a good place to see them is the monkey forest of Sangeh, next to the village, where the palahlar trees (*Dipterocarpus trinervis*, often mistakenly described as nutmeg trees) are up to 30–40 m (100–130 ft) high. Monkeys can be seen around a small temple, **Pura Bukit Sari**, deep in the woods but signposted on the main road. The monkeys are considered sacred, a tradition deriving from the Hindu *Ramayana* epic, in which Prince Rama allied himself with the monkey kings Subali and Hanoman to attack the evil king Rawana.

The monkeys – from a colony of around 700 grey long-tailed macaques – should be approached with caution. It is not advisable to get too friendly or the situation can quickly get out of hand. The monkeys may try to climb up on visitors' shoulders, and will not get down unless given something to eat, and while they are generally gentle, sociable creatures, panicky or brusque movements can provoke them to bite. The animals may even take spectacles, phones or money, in which case a *pawang* (monkey tamer) will retrieve the stolen object using a banana as an incentive.

Pura Bukit Sari

⊕ ⚐ Sangeh   ◷ 7:30am–6pm daily

15

Yeh Panas

🅰D3 🄰Penatahan, near Penebel 📞(0361) 262 356 🚌From Denpasar & Tabanan 🕑6am–8pm daily

It is worthwhile dropping by the Yeh Panas hot springs on the road to Gunung Batukaru from Tabanan or Penebel. The main hot springs have been turned into a spa, which also has a hotel; those which are open to the public are clearly indicated by signs. There is also a spring temple here.

Hot springs are also to be found in the village of Angsri near Apuan. They are in a pleasant, natural setting, but have no modern facilities.

16

Gunung Batukaru

🅰D2 🚌From Denpasar & Tabanan 🛈Tabanan; (0361) 811 602

Gunung Batukaru (also known as Batukau) is the second-highest peak in Bali after Gunung Agung. On its slopes is the last remaining true rainforest on the island. The mountain is much revered as the source of irrigation water for areas its south and west.

The temple of Pura Luhur Batukaru, with its shrine dedicated to the Lord of Gunung Batukaru and the goddess of nearby Lake Tamblingan (p165), is located among the lofty trees at its foot. There is a constant stream of worshippers performing rites or requesting holy water from the temple priests.

The charm of the temple's setting lies in a blend of artifice and nature: the spires of its *meru* shrines and other dark-thatched pavilions appear to have sprouted up among the greens of the trees, foliage and mosses. The name given to the central deity of the temple is Sang Hyang Tumuwuh, "The Ultimate Plant Grower".

To the east of Pura Luhur Batukaru on the Baturiti road are the famous rice terraces of Jatiluwih. Rice granaries line the road in the local villages. Other beautiful rice terraces can be seen in Pacung, at the turn-off to Jatiluwih and Batukaru.

17

Pura Gangga

🅰E3 🄰On a small road leading through Perean to Apuan and Baturiti 🛈Tabanan; (0361) 811 602

On the main highway to Bedugul, Pura Gangga temple is set on the lush banks of a small river. The temple has a seven-tier *meru* with a stone base. It is unusual in that the base is open at the front, rather than entirely closed in the usual fashion. Although the temple is not open to visitors, its atmospheric compound and architectural features can easily be viewed from outside the precincts.

Did You Know?

Pura Gangga is named after the holy river Ganges (Gangga) in India.

18

Perancak

🅰B2 🛈Negara; (0365) 41 060

The quiet Muslim village of Perancak, settled by migrating Madurese islanders, has a mosque with a tiered roof in the traditional Indonesian style and a tranquil, black-sand beach. The Madurese introduced their unique fishing boat designs to the area. Hidden up the Perancak river estuary, 10 km (6 miles) from Negara, you will find a "secret fleet" – a glittering armada of dozens of large, fully decked, high-prowed, traditional wooden vessels, known as *selerek*. Each boat is decorated with Hindu and Muslim iconography, multi-hued carvings and sculptures, crows' nests shaped like mythical winged chariots, flags and bunting, beads and mirrors. More of these colourful boats can be seen at the nearby atmospheric port of Pengambengan, where *dangdut* music blares from the dockside. *Dangdut* is an amalgamation of ethnic ensemble music combining Malay and Western elements together with Indian classic, pop and film music and urban Arab pop.

Negara

📍 B2 🚌 From Denpasar & Gilimanuk ℹ️ Jalan Ngurah Rai; (0365) 41 060

The real charm of Negara lies in the Bugis origin of its urban core. On both sides of the Ijo Gading River, south of the central bridge on Jalan Gatot Subroto, is the Bugis community of Loloan. A walk on its streets evokes the atmosphere of Sulawesi, from where many early Bugis migrants originated. Wooden houses with elaborately carved balconies line the streets. The most beautiful are at the end of Jalan Gunung Agung and on nearby Jalan Puncak Jaya. Loloan has several traditional *pesantren* (Islamic boarding schools).

Negara is also known for its *jegog*, gamelan orchestras playing huge bamboo instruments, and for the *makepung*, a sport which was introduced to West Bali by Madurese migrants from East Java. It is a race between two-wheeled chariots drawn by a pair of water buffaloes. The races, featuring Bali's

---

Gunung Batukaru viewed from rice fields near Pupuan

---

sleekest, most handsome buffaloes and most daring jockeys, are staged every year to please the god of the harvest.

A small road 4 km (2 miles) west of Negara leads to the quiet beach of Rening, 8 km (5 miles) away. From the nearby Cape Rening there is a beautiful sunset view over the mountains of eastern Java.

To the north are two Christian villages: Palasari (Catholic) and Blimbingsari (Protestant). These were established in the 1930s on state land given by the Dutch to Balinese converts to Christianity, who were excluded from their own community. The architecture in both is an interesting mix of Balinese and Dutch-Nordic styles.

THE NEGARA BUFFALO RACES

Held every July to November, the buffalo races see hundreds of pairs of bulls racing against each other at high speed along rice-field tracks. Festooned with bells, silks and decorative harnesses, each pair is hitched to a brightly painted wooden chariot, driven by a perilously balanced standing jockey. The race is an integral part of Bali life, but it has attracted criticism from animal rights groups.

↑ The Pura Rambut Siwi temple, near Medewi Beach

---

20 🍴

Medewi Beach

📍 C2 🚌 From Denpasar ℹ️ Negara; (0365) 41 060

Medewi is a beautiful rocky beach popular with surfers. The long, rolling breakers can be 7 m (23 ft) high. It tends to be quieter than many other surf hotspots due to being a little out of the way. The beach is composed of black sand, over which are scattered small black stones that glitter under the rays of the setting sun. On the horizon is the Javanese coast.

The **Pura Rambut Siwi** temple complex is built on a promontory, 6 km (4 miles) west of the beach. The setting offers a fine panorama over the sea. The main temple was established to venerate the priest Dang Hyang Nirartha, after he cured the local villagers of a deadly illness. There is a single, three-tiered *meru*. A lock of hair *(rambut),* believed to be the priest's, is kept as a relic in the pavilion shrine. The temple entrance faces the sea and is guarded by a statue of the demon queen Rangda. Entry is with a donation. There are other smaller temples in caves along the nearby cliff.

Pura Rambut Siwi

📍 6 km (4 miles) west of Medewi Beach ⏰ Daily

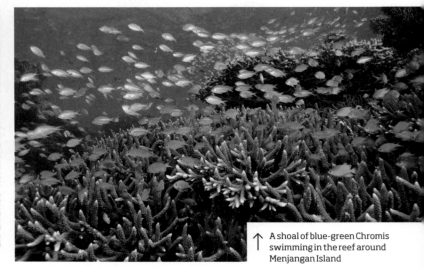

↑ A shoal of blue-green Chromis swimming in the reef around Menjangan Island

21

Gilimanuk

🅰 A1 🚌 From Denpasar & Singaraja 🚢 From Ketapang, Java 🛈 Negara; (0365) 41 060

Gilimanuk is the ferry port to Java. There are many *warung* here catering for travellers who sometimes have to wait hours for a ferry.

The main architectural feature is an enormous arched "gateway to Bali", topped by four flaming dragons facing in the cardinal directions, around a central throne of heaven.

North of Gilimanuk at Cekik, the **Museum Purbakala** (Archaeological Museum) displays some sarcophagi and Neolithic tools excavated from a nearby funerary site. Some promising archaeological discoveries have been made here showing signs of pre-Bronze Age human settlement in this area. Also in Cekik is the headquarters of the Taman Nasional Bali Barat *(p148)*, the nature reserve covering a substantial area of West Bali.

Museum Purbakala

  🅰 Jalan Raya 📞 (0365) 61 328 🕐 8am–6pm Mon-Fri

22

Makam Jayaprana

🅰 A1 🚩 Teluk Terima 🚌 From Denpasar & Seririt 🛈 Singaraja; (0362) 25 141 🕐 Daily

The Makam Jayaprana (Jayaprana Mausoleum) is also a temple. It is reached by a climb from the road; however, the panoramic view over Gunung Raung in Java, Menjangan Island and Gilimanuk is ample reward for the effort required to get there. The shrine was built on the burial site of Jayaprana, a romantic hero of Balinese folklore. According to legend, Jayaprana had married a woman named Layonsari, of such extreme beauty that the Lord of Kalianget decided to get rid of him and marry her. The king pretended that Bugis pirates had landed in Gilimanuk and sent Jayaprana with a body of soldiers to repel them. When they came to their destination the soldiers killed Jayaprana. However, resisting the advances of the king, Layonsari killed herself to rejoin her beloved Jayaprana in death. Today, suitors ask for favours of love at the grave. It is decorated with statues of Jayaprana and Layonsari.

23

Menjangan Island

🅰 A1 🚌 To Labuhan Lalang from Denpasar & Seririt 🚢 From Labuhan Lalang 🛈 Labuhan Lalang; (0365) 61 060

For those who wish to dive and snorkel in a pristine environment, Menjangan Island is not to be missed. Technically part of the Taman Nasional Bali Barat *(p148)*, it owes its name to the Java deer *(menjangan)*, which swim across from the mainland. There are eight main diving points around the island, each with its own marine

Did You Know?

Pemuteran is home to the world's largest coral-reef restoration project.

life. The best is perhaps the Anchor Wreck, named for the encrusted anchor on the reef.

Labuhan Lalang, on the bay of Teluk Terima, is Bali's nearest point of access to Menjangan Island. Boat tickets may be bought at the office of the Department of Forestry here. The last boats leave for Menjangan Island at 11am and return at dusk. There is basic accommodation at Labuhan Lalang.

㉔ Pemuteran

🅐 B1 🚌 ℹ️ Singaraja; (0362) 25 141

A coastal resort and fishing village, with plenty of accommodation options, Pemuteran has beautiful coral reefs with a profusion of tropical fish. There are good diving and snorkelling spots, and a turtle sanctuary. It is a convenient place for visitors to Menjangan Island to stay overnight; a boat can be rented here. Some hotels offer early-morning dolphin-spotting excursions.

→

Pilgrims on the steps of Pura Pulaki, a Hindu temple near Pemuteran

A little west of Pemuteran is the small Banyuwedang Bay. The name is Balinese for "hot springs". There are many springs along this shore, supposedly with curative powers. They are alternately covered and exposed by the tide.

Pura Pulaki, about 5 km (3 miles) east of Pemuteran, is a coastal temple near a point where a mountain ridge plunges abruptly into the sea, almost blocking the coastal passage. It is associated with the Shaivite priest Dang Hyang Nirartha, who is said to have turned the local inhabitants into *gamang* (ghosts). Living around it are mischievous monkeys; they are regarded as holy.

Atlas South Sea Pearl Farm, 10 km (6 miles) east of Pemuteran, conducts tours, including a demonstration of pearl seeding and harvesting. The pearls are made into fine pieces of jewellery and exported worldwide.

Guided tours of the **Hatten Wines Vineyard**, 13 km (8 miles) east of Pemuteran, include a visit to the laboratory and demonstrations of the different stages of wine production, followed by a wine tasting.

Pura Pulaki

 🏠 Banyu Poh 🕐 Daily

Atlas South Sea Pearl Farm

🏠 Penyabangan 🌐 atlaspearls.com.au/pages/visit-a-pearl-farm

Hatten Wines Vineyard

🏠 Sanggalangit 🕐 9am–8pm daily 🌐 hatten wines.com

㉕ Pantai Gondol

🅐 B1 📍 6 km (4 miles) west of Gerokgak, across the field next to the Fisheries Research Project (Perikanan) 🚌 ℹ️ Singaraja; (0362) 25 141

The beautiful, serene white-sand Gondol beach is located at the foot of a small promontory, the Gondol Cape. With stunning coral, it is a good, uncrowded spot for snorkelling and diving.

26
Banjar

🅰D1 🚌To Seririt, then own transport ℹ️Singaraja; (0362) 25 141

Set on the coastal plain with the North Bali uplands as a backdrop, Banjar is a town of historic significance. In 1871, when still a semi-independent kingdom run by a Brahman family, it put up strong resistance to Dutch encroachment during the Banjar War. The ruling family was eliminated in one of Bali's first recorded *puputan*, or mass ritual suicide in preference to surrender.

The Brahmans from Banjar are famous for their literary talents. In the 19th century they adapted texts from classical Kawi (Old Javanese) into common Balinese.

Brahma Vihara Arama is a Buddhist monastery built in 1970 by a powerful local Brahman, Bhikku Giri Rakhita, who converted to Theravada Buddhism, the form of Buddhism prevalent in Thailand. Visitors are welcome, but overnight rooms are only available for participants in meditation courses.

Another highlight of the town is the **Banjar Hot Springs**, which are popular with both locals and visitors from nearby Lovina. Entry is with a donation. There are three pools; in the highest one the water is hot. Eight carved dragon-heads spurt out greenish-yellow, sulphurous water believed to have therapeutic properties. The hot water is considered sacred by the locals – a temple has been built around the spring, which is set in cool and lush environs.

From Banjar it is worth visiting Pedawa, 10 km (6 miles) inland. This remote place is a Bali Aga village. It was one of the villages which rebelled against the Javanese occupation of 1343, and has retained Hindu cultural features dating from before that time. Indeed, the Hindu

> **The Brahmans from Banjar are famous for their literary talents. In the 19th century they adapted texts from classical Kawi (Old Javanese) into common Balinese.**

triad of Brahma-Vishnu-Shiva was unknown here until recently. While the Balinese generally build a range of shrines for gods and ancestors behind their houses, the people of Pedawa build a single bamboo structure.

There are two routes from Banjar to Pedawa: both run through stunning mountain and plantation landscapes.

In Sidatapa, another Bali Aga village 8 km (5 miles) from Banjar, some interesting old houses made of bamboo still remain. This is one of the oldest villages in North Bali, dating to the first century AD.

Brahma Vihara Arama

♽ ⊛ 🏠 Between Banjar and Pedawa 🕗8am–6pm daily 🌐brahmaviharaarama.com

Banjar Hot Springs

🏠Jalan Banjar 🕗8am–6pm daily 🌐banjarhotspring.co.id

Bathers at the Banjar Hot Springs, and *(inset)* detail of dragon-head spouts ↓

EXPERIENCE North and West Bali

Munduk

 D2 From Singaraja & Seririt Singaraja; (0362) 25141

Munduk is a highland village amid plantations of coffee and cloves. It is set on a high ridge near the volcanic lakes of Tamblingan, Buyan and Bratan. In the area there are still a few resthouses from the 1920s, built in a mixed Dutch colonial-Chinese style. In the village it is possible to visit the workshop of I Made Trip, Bali's most famous maker of bamboo instruments.

Munduk is an ideal base for exploring on rented bicycles, for mountain walks to Pedawa, for rice-field walks to Uma Jero, or for a tour of Lake Tamblingan and Lake Bratan. There are several waterfalls in the area – the most impressive are 30 m (100 ft) high, and can be found 1 km (half a mile) along the road eastwards to Bedugul. The path down to the waterfall is dense with clove and coffee trees.

↑ Harvesting hydrangeas in the fields surrounding Lake Tamblingan

point is arched by the roots of a huge bunutan tree. Blimbing, 12 km (7 miles) to the south, has the nearest accommodation, panoramic views and a restaurant.

 INSIDER TIP
Walking

Avoid rainy season (Oct-Apr) when the trails around the lake are slippery. The forest paths are narrow and the undergrowth can be up to 2 m (7 ft) high. In dry season it is easy to negotiate the route.

---

(28)

Pupuan

D2 From Denpasar & Singaraja Tabanan; (0361) 811 602

Situated in the rainiest part of the whole island, Pupuan is Bali's vegetable-growing centre. The area around it is cool and mountainous. The road from Seririt to Antosari travels through some of Bali's most beautiful landscape, with excellent coastal views. It climbs steeply via Busungbiu, Pupuan and through a forested pass 790 m (2,600 ft) high into lush spice-growing countryside. It then winds down to Blimbing and Bajra before passing rice terraces, with rice barns along the road. The road southwest towards Pekutatan passes a coffee plantation area, and at one

---

(29)

Lake Tamblingan

D2 From Bedugul or Munduk

A scenic road follows the rim of the massive Catur Caldera overlooking the northern shores of Lake Buyan and

↑ A road through the roots of a huge bunutan tree near Pupuan

Lake Tamblingan. Rustic bamboo viewing stations line the road, and the views are awe-inspiring. For an experience of being close to nature, trek through the ancient rainforest, which is accessed via a flight of stone steps on the shoulder of land between the two lakes. The forest resounds with birdsong, and you may spot babblers, woodpeckers, ground thrushes and malkohas. The pathways lead to a clearing beside Lake Tamblingan, next to Pura Tahun, a temple with an 11-roofed *meru*. Motorboats and watersports are forbidden, but you may arrange for a boatman to row you across the lake in a *pedau akit*, a traditional double canoe, to the tiny village of Munduk Tamblingan, where you will find Pura Gubug (the Farmers' Temple), dedicated to the lake goddess.

30

Lake Buyan

D2 From Singaraja
Singaraja; (0362) 25 141

There are great views over the lake from the mountain road – dense forest scrub vanishes at the shoreline into the water. Boats can be hired from local fishers and treks organized to a cave on the slopes of Gunung Lesong, to Gesing or to Munduk.

31

Lake Bratan and Bedugul

E2 From Singaraja & Denpasar Tabanan; (0361) 811 602

The main attraction in the mountain-lake resort of Bedugul, Lake Bratan offers water activities such as parasailing and water-skiing. Visitors can hire boats, and there are guides for treks to peaks such as Gunung Catur and Gunung Puncak Manggu. The lake is the setting for the 17th-century Pura Ulun Danu Bratan temple, built on a small island and dedicated to the goddess of the lake, Dewi Danu. There is a small

stupa-shaped shrine for Buddhist worshippers, with statues of Buddhas occupying niches that mark the four points of the compass. The panorama includes an 11-tiered *meru* located on the shore across a wooden bridge.

Elsewhere in Bedugal, the 1.5 sq km (0.6 sq m) **Bali Botanic Garden** contains 320 species of orchids, a fern garden, a herbarium and plants used for making *jamu* (traditional medicines).

North of Lake Bratan, the well-kept Bali Handara Kosaido Country Club has a world-class golf course *(www.handaragolfresort.com)*.

Bali Botanic Garden

 Kebun Raya, west of Candi Kuning Daily krbali.lipi.go.id

32

Lovina

D1 Kalibukbuk; (0362) 41 910

The long stretch of coast encompassing several villages, from Tukadmungga in the east to Kaliasem in the west, is

collectively known as Lovina. The beach resort area has quiet, black-sand coves lined with coconut trees. Outriggers add to the nostalgic charm, and are available for early-morning dolphin-watching excursions. For snorkellers, there are pristine coral reefs.

The tourist facilities of Lovina are on Jalan Binaria, which leads to a modern sculpture of dolphins. From the village of Temukus, it is possible to trek to the Singsing Waterfall.

33

Jagaraga

E1 From Singaraja
Singaraja; (0362) 25 141

Jagaraga was the site of a battle in 1849, in which Patih Jelantik, the prime minister of the state of Buleleng, held the

The beautiful Gitgit waterfall surrounded by tropical rainforest

Dutch to a long stand-off before he was defeated. The relationship between the Balinese and the Dutch is reflected in the lively reliefs of the local temple of the dead, **Pura Dalem**. These were carved in the early decades of the 20th century. The subjects include aircraft, ships and a European in a car being held up by an armed man.

The central gate of Pura Beji in Sangsit, 4 km (3 miles) northwest of Jagaraga, is famous for its ornamentation. Garudas (mythical birds) are carved half in the round, half in low relief. The nearby Pura Dalem has some grim depictions of the tortures in hell inflicted on those who infringe moral rules.

The country around Sawan, 4 km (3 miles) south of Jagaraga, is said to produce some of Bali's best rice. There are impressive river gorges in the area. Sawan is also known for its northern dance and music tradition.

About 12 km (8 miles) east of Sangsit, Air Sanih is a small beach resort named after a

spring feeding a natural pool, which is great for swimming. There is a beach restaurant and basic accommodation.

Pura Dalem
⊘ ⊗ ⬚ Jagaraga ⊙ Daily

 Gitgit

⬚ D1 🚌 From Singaraja & Bedugul 🛈 Singaraja; (0362) 25 141

This village is the location of an impressive waterfall, 45 m (149 ft) high, about 400 m (450 yds) from the main road and surrounded by lush vegetation. Another waterfall, 1 km (half a mile) up the hill, is not quite as high, but there are fewer visitors there.

Pegayaman, just north of Gitgit, maintains 17th-century Javanese traditions. On the

Prophet's birthday, Muslim villagers parade a *tumpeng* (mountain-shaped offering).

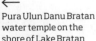 **Tejakula**

⬚ F1 🚌 From Singaraja 🛈 Singaraja; (0362) 25 141

The old village of Tejakula is famous for its silver jewellery and its ancient *wayang wong* traditional dance. This eastern part of the regency of Buleleng is one of the most unspoiled areas of Bali. At Tejakula itself there are some quiet black beaches and idyllic coconut groves.

Nearby are several Bali Aga villages. One of them, Sembiran (a short way up the mountain road west of Tejakula), has the characteristic stone-paved roads, some megalithic remains and good views down to the north coast.

A pleasant walk upriver, 8 km (5 miles) east of Tejakula, leads to the mighty Yeh Mempeh (Flying Water) waterfall.

Pura Ulun Danu Bratan water temple on the shore of Lake Bratan

LOMBOK

The Sasaks are the Indigenous people of Lombok. Numbering about three million, they are thought to be descended from a hill tribe of North India and Myanmar. The minority Balinese population, about 100,000, live mostly near the west coast.

Lombok's identity has been formed by two major influences. Javanese arrivals in the 14th century brought Islam and Middle-Eastern influences, while the Balinese Hindus, who were the colonial masters of the island from the 16th century until the 1890s, have been an important presence. These groups give the island a rich heritage of dialects and languages, traditional dance, music, rituals and crafts.

Lombok appeals to visitors for its natural beauty more than for its architectural heritage. The island's varied geography provides ideal conditions for trekking, surfing and windsurfing, diving, snorkelling and game fishing. However, like Bali, Lombok sits on the so-called "ring of fire", and devastating earthquakes in July and August 2018 killed over 500 and caused inestimable damage. Thousands of tourists on the Gili Islands and Mount Rinjani had to be evacuated.

LOMBOK

Must Sees

1 Taman Nasional Gunung Rinjani
2 Gili Islands
3 Mataram

Experience More

4 Lembar
5 Narmada
6 Senggigi
7 Tanjung
8 Segenter
9 Sembalun
10 Bayan Beleq Mosque
11 Sapit
12 Senaru
13 Labuhan Lombok
14 Pringgasela
15 Tetebatu
16 Rembitan and Sade
17 Gerupuk
18 Sukarara
19 Penujak
20 Kuta
21 Tanjung Aan Beach
22 Mawun Beach
23 Bangko Bangko
24 Selong Blanak
25 Tanjung Luar
26 Banyumulek
27 Southwestern Gili Islands

Indian Ocean

Bali Sea

LOMBOK

Sukadana

SEGENTER **8**

Kayangan

BAYAN BELEQ **10**
MOSQUE

Putih

Beburung

Pedamekan

Belanting

Gili Lawang

Gili Sulat

Tiuteja Waterfall

Dasansantong

12 SENARU

Sajang

Bawaknaw

Lendangbatu

Sendanggile Waterfalls

Gubukrempung

Gunung Senkereang Jaya
2,902 m (9,520 ft)

9 SEMBALUN

Danau Segara Anak

Gunung Rinjani
3,726 m (12,224 ft)

Gunung Nangi
2,330 m (7,644 ft)

Maroak

TAMAN NASIONAL
GUNUNG RINJANI **1**

Gubuktambak

Nasional *Gunung* *Rinjani*

Menangabaris

Pesugulan

11 SAPIT

13 LABUHAN
LOMBOK

Otakgawar

Jeruk Manis Waterfall

Suwela

TETEBATU **15**

Pringgabaya

L O M B O K

PRINGGASELA **14**

Aikmel

Mantang

Loyok

Masbagik

Kopang

Montongbaan

Selong

Alas Strait

Penden

Sakra

Praya

Gunungrajak

Labuhan
Haji

Bendungan Batujat

Batunyale

19 PENUJAK

Orokorok

Beleka

Sepit

Palung

✈
Lombok
International Airport

Mujur

Ganti

Tangun

25 TANJUNG LUAR

Sengkol

Pengembur

Pemokong

16 REMBITAN
AND SADE

Batu
Nampar

Pengorosdalam

Tanjung Ringgit

TANJUNG
AAN BEACH

Ekas Bay

20
KUTA

21

17 GERUPUK

0 kilometres   10

0 miles   10

N

① 🥾 🏔️

TAMAN NASIONAL GUNUNG RINJANI

🅰️ C4 🚌 to Anyar, then *bemo* to Senaru; to Aikmel, then *bemo* to Sembalu ℹ️ Mataram; www.rinjaninationalpark.com

At 3,726 m (12,224 ft) high, Gunung Rinjani volcano towers over the landscape of Lombok and plays an important role in the religions and folklore of both the Hindus and Sasaks of the island.

The mountain and its satellites form the Taman Nasional Gunung Rinjani (Mount Rinjani National Park), a magnet for experienced trekkers and nature lovers. The main entry points to the park are via Senaru or Sembalun villages. Within Mount Rinjani's huge caldera are the stunning Segara Anak crater lake, the Aik Kalak hot springs and the small active cone of Gunung Baru. Hindus and Sasaks regard the mountain (the second-tallest volcano in Indonesia after Mount Kerinci on Sumatra) as sacred, and make pilgrimages to the summit and lake to leave offerings to the gods and spirits.

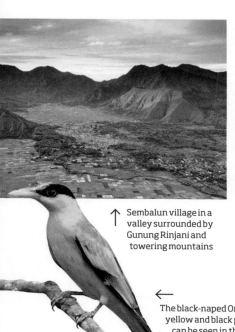

↑ Sembalun village in a valley surrounded by Gunung Rinjani and towering mountains

 INSIDER TIP
Trekking

Guides are mandatory. The easiest and safest way to organize a visit is through a trekking agency in Mataram, Senggigi or Senaru (prices include return transport). Typically, a trek to the crater rim takes two days and one night. The longer and more strenuous ascent to the summit is usually part of a three- to four-day trek. June to August are the best months as they are the driest. Take warm clothing as it can be extremely cold at the rim and summit.

← The black-naped Oriole, with yellow and black plumage, can be seen in the park

↑ Gunung Baru in the blue-green waters of Lake Segara Anak in the crater rim, and *(inset)* trekking to Mount Rinjani from Sembalun

② 🍴 🍽️

GILI ISLANDS

🏝️ A–B4 🚐 From Senggigi & Mataram to Bangsal 🚤 From Bangsal
or from Benoa Harbour, Sanur and Amed in Bali ℹ️ Mataram;
(0370) 637 828

Lying off the northwest coast of Lombok, the three small islands
known as the Gili Islands form some of Lombok's most spectacular
natural beauty and are a major tourist destination. Especially popular
with divers, the waters around the islands teem with tropical marine
life and have good visibility all year round.

These idyllic islands were "discovered" by
backpackers in the 1980s, who fell in love with
the crystal-clear waters, full of all manner of
colourful marine life, and the pure white-sand
beaches. Simple bungalows with generator-
supplied electricity soon sprang up to cater to
a crowd eager to get off the beaten track. The
popularity of the islands has been growing
steadily since 2005 when the first direct fastboat service was introduced, cutting travel
time from Bali by more than half. Since
then, the development of upmarket hotels,
restaurants and dive centres has taken
place at a rapid rate.

The Lombok earthquakes in July and
August 2018 struck the Gili Islands, wreaking
significant structural damage and temporarily
halting tourism. However, hotel, restaurant,
and dive-centre owners were quick to repair
and rebuild, and the Gili Islands are open for
business once again.

Motorized transport is banned from all three
islands. Transport comprises horse-drawn
carts called *cidomos*, or bicycles which can
be hired by the hour or by the day.

↑ Orange-and-white striped clownfish
in the waters off the Gili islands

← Aerial view of the coastline of Gili Air, and *(inset)* sun rising behind Mount Rinjani seen from Gili Air

> **GREAT VIEW**
> **Mandarinfish**
>
> If you dive in the Gili Air Harbour at sunset, you may get to see the rare and mesmerizing Mandarinfish with its respendent colours - one of the most beautiful fish in the ocean.

GILI AIR

Meaning "Little Island of Water", Gili Air is the island closest to the Lombok mainland and the most easily accessed of the three Gilis. While the bars here aren't as loud as on Gili Trawangan, there are still plenty of opportunities to have fun. Most of the development on Gili Air is on the east coast, facing Lombok and the towering Mount Rinjani. From here there are spectacular sunrises, while sunsets behind Mount Agung on Bali are visible from the south and western coasts.

The best beaches are on the south or east side, with clear turquoise waters and soft white sand. Diving facilities abound and there is good snorkelling directly from the shore, particularly from the east and northeast beaches. Gili Air Wall, off the west coast, is a popular dive site, with soft corals gleaming yellow and orange in the sunlight. Here you can see harbour scorpion fish and thousands of glassfish, turtles and, if you look very carefully, tiny pigmy seahorses hiding in the sea fans. In the deeper waters are whitetip reef sharks and schools of larger fish species. Hahn's Reef is a superb training site for beginners. With the right conditions, there are good waves off the south of the island, which attract surfers.

↑ A typical traditional wooden house in a village on Gili Air

GILI TRAWANGAN

The furthest from the mainland and the largest of the three Gili islands, yet small enough to walk around in an hour and a half, Gili Trawangan is known as "the party island", yet has a wide range of attractions and facilities to suit a broad spectrum of visitors. Despite the many restaurants and lounge bars lining the shores of its powdery white-sand beaches, it's still possible to find a quiet stretch of beach to enjoy undisturbed, especially on the north and west coasts, while peaceful inland villages provide an experience of rural life. Behind the glitz and glamour, a laidback bohemian atmosphere still prevails.

As well as plenty of backpacker rooms there are many glamorous boutique bungalows, hotels, resorts and private-pool villas. All have been constructed in harmony with the islands' local charms – natural materials and simple elegance are the dominant themes of most developments. There are no high-rise hotels, and definitely no tour buses or fast-food chains, but plenty of dive centres to help visitors explore the islands' fabulous coral reefs.

Gili Trawangan is the island that offers the best choice of activities, including some superb spa facilities, horse-riding stables, sea kayaks for rent, and what claims to be the smallest public cinema in the world, where you can laze on floor cushions and watch newly released movies. There is good snorkelling just off the shore. Strong currents are sometimes a bother, however, especially in the strait with neighbouring Gili Meno. Further out are vast gardens of coral, regarded as one of the best dive spots in Lombok, particularly Shark Point to the east of the island, which is home to a huge number of fish, whitetip reef sharks and green and hawksbill turtles. The hill in the south of the island is a great lookout from which to enjoy the spectacular sunset views across the ocean to Bali; or in the mornings, the brilliant sunrise over Mount Rinjani on Lombok.

↑ Open-sided beach hut on Gili Trawangan, a tropical paradise

💬 **INSIDER TIP**
Snorkelling

Masks, snorkels and fins can easily be hired. Wearing rubber shoes can make it easier to get into the water. Currents can cause you to drift so you will need to walk back to where you started. Snorkelling trips in glass-bottomed boats can be arranged on Gili Trawangan along the main strip. A highlight of snorkelling here is that you are very likely to see green and hawksbill turtles.

→ Visitors cycling on rented bikes in palm forest on Gili Meno, the smallest of the islands

MARINE LIFE IN THE GILI ISLANDS

Divers of all levels of ability will find a rich variety of reef fish and other underwater life. Those who want to see sharks can generally do so within a day's diving off the Gili Islands, especially reef sharks, which have no interest in humans. The coral is fine, despite damage caused by fishbombing and earthquakes in past years. You can spot the orange-and-white striped clownfish, the brightly coloured parrotfish and the majestic Moorish idol in the waters around the Gilis. There are also endangered green turtles and hawksbills turtles living in these waters.

GILI MENO

Positioned in the middle, Gili Meno is the smallest of the three Gili Islands. It also has the lowest population – just a few hundred residents. Gili Meno is not as developed as Gili Trawangan or Gili Air, and the pace here is slower. The landscape is flat, with coconut groves inland, and a small and shallow saltwater lake in the west from which the local people harvest meagre supplies of salt during the dry season. The main activities for visitors are yoga, snorkelling and scuba diving. Gili Meno Wall, off the west coast, is a popular dive site, with giant gorgonian fans and many varieties of marine life. Hawksbill and green turtles inhabit the waters around Gili Meno, particularly on the northwest corner, and the reefs just offshore feature outcrops of brilliant blue coral. The best place f or snorkelling, meanwhile, is at Blue Coral Point off the northeast coast, where the reef showcases numerous species of coral and colourful fish. At night, divers can witness huge Moray eels, entertaining Spanish dancers, baby cuttlefish and a whole array of crustaceans. At the turtle nursery on Meno, the hatchlings are kept in holding tanks until they are large and healthy enough to be released into the sea. Visitors can take part in this release programme. Small donations are welcome.

③

MATARAM

🅰B5 🚌Sweta ℹDepartment of Tourism, Art & Culture,
Jalan Singosari 2; (0370) 632 723 or (0370) 634 800

Lombok's capital is an urban sprawl of several towns –
Mataram, Ampenan and Cakranegara – merged
together without a break. The city is characterized
by parks and wide, tree-lined streets with buildings
which echo traditional Sasak styles.

The city's large, whitewashed, high-roofed houses hark back to Dutch colonial days. Ampenan, to the west, was Lombok's main port and a vital link in the spice trade at that time. Its old winding streets are lined with shops and restaurants. Some of the buildings show an Art Deco influence. At night, food carts and *warungs* sell inexpensive, tasty food. It also has a colourful Arab quarter. To the east of Ampenan is Mataram, Lombok's administrative centre, with government buildings, mosques and a university. Further east, Cakranegara was the royal capital until a century ago. It is home to many Chinese and Balinese and is today the main business and shopping area, with stores selling gold, textiles and clothing.

↑ The three elegant multi-tiered shrines at Pura Meru

①
Museum Negeri Nusa Tenggara Barat

🏠Jalan Panji Tilar Negara 6
📞(0370) 632 159 🕐8am-11am Fri (to 3pm Sat-Thu)
🚫Public hols

This museum displays locally made textiles, ceramics, woodcarvings and copperwork, as well as artifacts relating to the islands of West Nusa Tenggara and paintings representing different cultures.

②
Pura Meru

🏠Jalan Selaparang, Cakranegara 🕐Daily

With its three slender *meru* representing the Hindu gods Vishnu, Shiva and Brahma, this is Lombok's largest Hindu temple complex. Built in the early 18th century, it consists of an inner courtyard with many small shrines. The central eleven-tiered *meru* is Shiva's house; the nine-tiered *meru* is Vishnu's home; and the seven-tiered meru is Brahma's abode.

③
Mayura Water Palace

🏠Jalan Selaparang, Cakranegara 📞(0370) 624 442 🕐Daily

Built in 1844 under the Balinese Karangasem dynasty, this complex includes the former king's family temple. The centrepiece is a lake, surrounded by a park dotted with shrines and fountains.

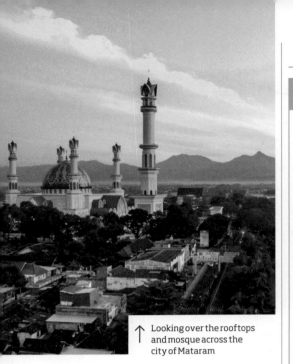

↑ Looking over the rooftops and mosque across the city of Mataram

④

Pura Lingsar

🏠 Off Jalan Gora II ⏰ 7am–6pm daily

Some 6 km (4 miles) northeast of Mataram in the village of Lingsar, the large Pura Lingsar temple complex was built in 1714 and is nestled in beautiful rice fields. A multi-denominational site, it has a temple for Balinese Hindus (Pura Gaduh), as well as one for Lombok's form of Islam – Wetu Telu. The Wetu Telu temple is noted for its enclosed lily-covered pond and for the holy eels, which can be enticed from hiding (it is considered good luck to feed them) with hard-boiled eggs, which are available for purchase at stalls. Entry to the complex is with a donation.

WETU TELU

A mixture of Hindu, Islamic and Indigenous animist beliefs, Wetu Telu is the traditional religion of the Sasak people in Lombok and is officially a sect of Islam. This mystical religion centres on a physical concept of the Holy Trinity: the sun, moon and stars represent heaven, earth and water; the head, body and limbs creativity, sensitivity and control. Unlike most Muslims, followers of Wetu Telu (which means "Three Times") pray three times a day instead of five times, do not fast for the full month of Ramadan and can consume alcohol such as rice wine.

Another more orthodox form of Islam in Lombok is Wetu Lima (meaning "Five Times"). Under Suharto's government in the 1960s, Indigenous beliefs such as Wetu Telu were discouraged and today it is mainly practised in the traditional northern heartland of Bayan.

EXPERIENCE MORE

❹ Lembar

🅰️A5 🚌⛴️From Padang Bai & Benoa Harbour
ℹ️In ferry terminal

Lombok's main sea port, in a bay surrounded by hills, is the gateway to the island for passenger car-ferries from Bali. Crowds of merchants and other travellers mill around Lembar's ferry terminus. Much lively haggling takes place over prices of seats in over-loaded buses and vans travelling to other destinations on Lombok. There is a small tourist office, some phones and a few food stalls. At the docks, beautiful Bugis schooners and small steamers load and unload cargo.

The roads around Lembar run through lush, rural scenery. The coast road, skirting the peninsula towards Sekotong some 10 km (6 miles) to the south, has good views of the bay and its *bagan*, stationary fishing platforms standing in the sea. Fishers lower huge nets into which they attract fish with the aid of lanterns. From here skiffs take passengers to the remote coral islands of Gili Gede and Gili Nanggu.

---

❺ Narmada

🅰️B5 🚌 ℹ️Mataram; (0370) 632 723 or 634 800
🕐Daily

Built in 1805, Narmada was originally a raja's (king's) summer palace. In the gardens is a temple and a lake said to represent the crater lake of Gunung Rinjani. The lotus-filled ponds and terraced gardens recall royal splendours of the past.

---

❻ Senggigi

🅰️A5 🚌From Lembar & Mataram ℹ️Mataram; (0370) 632 723 or 634 800

Senggigi was once the most popular resort in Lombok, but most tourists now prefer to head for the Gili Islands. Although it's much less developed than Kuta in Bali, Senggigi has a broad range of accom-modation, restaurants and entertainment facilities.

Senggigi Beach is, strictly speaking, two glistening bays, separated by a thrust

EAT

Remajah Indah 2
Feast on super fresh seafood at this no-frills restaurant in Lembar. The spicy prawns and crab served here are crowd-favourites.

🅰️A5 📍Jalan Raya Lembar Serumbung 8, Lembar 📞(0819) 1721 0212

💲💲💲

Square Restaurant
This fine-dining restaurant serves European and local cuisine. Choose from curries, satays and Western favourites.

🅰️A5 📍Jalan Raya Senggigi km 8, Senggigi Square, Blok B-10, Senggigi
🌐squarelombok.com

💵💵💵

Café Alberto
This chic restaurant serves perfectly prepared Italian and Indonesian dishes on an open-air patio perched between a swimming pool and the beach.

🅰️A5 📍Jalan Raya Senggigi, Batu Bolong
🌐cafealberto.com

💵💵💵

↑ The Miru Temple, set within the grounds of Narmada

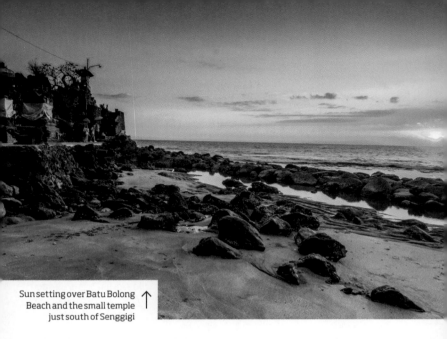

Sun setting over Batu Bolong Beach and the small temple just south of Senggigi ↑

of white coral jutting out into the ocean, but the area officially known as Senggigi is a 6-km (4-mile) strip of road and beachfront. Restaurants and cafés line the colourful main beach road.

The views up and down the coast, and out across the sea to Bali, which can be enjoyed from the coastal road, are majestic. Swimming off the beach is safe; and waves suitable for less experienced wave-riders peel to the left and right off the reef. Many people also windsurf here. Around the reef itself is a variety of marine life and beautiful coral. This is a good spot for relaxed snorkelling.

An atmospheric temple shrine stands on a black outcrop of rock reaching out

> **Tanjung is surrounded by lush countryside in which coconut groves alternate with picturesque rice fields and vegetable gardens.**

into the sea at Batu Bolong Beach, 3 km (2 miles) south of central Senggigi. The crimson sunsets are beautiful.

 Tanjung

🅰 B4 🚌 From Mataram
ℹ Mataram; (0370) 632 723 or 634 800

Tanjung's livelihood is based on fishing as well as agricultural products. It is a large village on the road north to the Gunung Rinjani foothills, with a twice-weekly cattle market. Tanjung is surrounded by lush countryside in which coconut groves alternate with picturesque ricefields and vegetable gardens. In the river shallows grows *kangkung* (a leafy vegetable rather like watercress), one of Lombok's most popular side dishes.

The road north from Tanjung runs along the black-sand beach and the terrain becomes distinctly arid. Some 4 km (2 miles) away on the coast is Krakas, famous for fresh, cool spring water. The spring is located underwater

400 m (1,320 ft) offshore at a depth of about 10 m (33 ft). Further north, just past the small town of Gondang, are the Tiu Pupas waterfall and seven caves.

 Segenter

🅰 B4 🚌 From Mataram
ℹ Mataram; (0370) 632 723 or 634 800

Segenter is a typical Sasak village. The settlement is made up of traditional bamboo and reed dwellings. Situated between these houses are *berugak* – open-air, thatched structures, set above ground level. It is usually used to receive guests. In the late morning, you'll see many villagers resting in their *berugak*, greeting passersby.

The people of Segenter produce most of the staple food necessary for their daily needs and plant cotton, rice and tobacco to sell at the market. Visit the village to learn more about Sasak culture.

Did You Know?

Sembalun is a traditional weaving community known for its beautiful textiles.

Sembalun

C4 From Mataram & Tanjung Mataram; (0370) 632 723 or 634 800

Lying in a valley surrounded by mountains is Sembalun, a village consisting of single-storey wooden buildings. Visitors are few, and there are only a couple of basic places to stay. There is a pleasant sense of remoteness. The air is fresh, and can be quite cold at night. This is a good place for walks. Shallots are grown here, and a pungent, but not unpleasant, scent pervades the valley.

From here the view of Gunung Rinjani is very vivid: the mountain seems to be almost within an arm's reach. Sembalun is the starting point of a Rinjani climb route more direct than that from Senaru, but the facilities here are not as good.

The road south to Sapit runs across one of the highest mountain passes in Indonesia. The hairpins and gradients give good views over the Sembalun Valley.

Bayan Beleq Mosque

C4 Beleq, Karang Bajo, Bayan

The oldest mosque on Lombok, this enchanting building near Beleq village was founded by Syeh Gaus Abdul Razak in 1634. It is comprised of a black sugar-palm fibre roof, decorated with a wooden crown, and woven bamboo walls resting upon a low stone wall. The natural materials have to be renewed every six years. The *meru*-shaped roof typifies the Javanese/Hindu influence that preceded Islam. Beside the mosque are the graves of some of the early followers of Wetu Telu, the syncretic Sasak form of Islam. The mosque is only used for religious ceremonies three times per year; at other times, visitors who wish to enter must speak to the caretaker.

Sapit

C4 From Sweta Mataram; (0370) 632 723 or 634 800

Sapit is situated on the eastern slopes of Gunung Rinjani at about 800 m (2,640 ft) above sea level. It is a refreshingly cool mountain resort commanding views of eastern Lombok, and of Sumbawa across the sea beyond. Blanketing Rinjani's lower slopes around Sapit are emerald-green rice terraces and tobacco plantations.

The village is basic, but gardens and flowerbeds make a fresh, orderly impression. There are some good, inexpensive guesthouses here.

Senaru

C4 From Sweta & Tanjung Mataram; (0370) 632 723 or 634 800

At a height of over 400 m (1,320 ft) on the lower slopes of Gunung Rinjani, Senaru is braced by cool, refreshing air. From here the visitor is rewarded with perfect views of Rinjani to the south and the ocean to the west.

Once a secluded mountain settlement sheltered from the outside world, this village, with its traditional-style houses, has become a weekend escape from the heat of the coastal regions. With its many simple guesthouses and restaurants, it is the most popular departure

→ The breathtaking Tiu Kelep waterfall on the outskirts of Senaru

point for treks and climbs up the mountain. It is also possible to make arrangments for a trek through the Gunung Rinjani national park and up the volcano. Camping equipment, tent and sleeping-bag rental are available, porters and guides can be engaged and food and other necessities can be bought here.

An easy 30-minute walk to the west of Senaru leads to the dramatic 40 m- (132 ft-) high Sendanggile Waterfalls, where water comes straight off one of the highest peaks in Southeast Asia. Here is the chance to wade in what must be the cleanest and freshest water in Indonesia. A little further uphill is the Tiu Kelep waterfall, with a lovely pool perfect for swimming.

Another short 30-minute walk from the village centre is Payan, which has thatched huts and a megalithic appearance: this is one of Lombok's few remaining Wetu Telu villages. Although somewhat commercialized, it is an example of Lombok's ancestral village traditions. Wetu Telu is a form of

← Hikers climbing Gunung Rinjani in the national park at Sembalun

Islam mixing Islamic beliefs with pre-Islamic Indigenous and Hindu-Buddhist elements. The Muslim practices observed at Payan contain both Balinese and Hindu elements. The women wear traditional sarongs and black shirts for weaving and during Muslim ceremonies.

13

Labuhan Lombok

⊞ C5 🚌 From Mataram ⛴ From Mataram and Sumbawa 🛈 In ferry terminal

The bay around Labuhan Lombok forms a natural harbour. There are good views of Gunung Rinjani from here. A road runs parallel with the shore, and between it and the waterside are the settlements of Bugis fishers consisting of houses on stilts. Colourfully painted trawlers are moored nearby. The forebears of this community came from South Sulawesi. The town's Sunday market sells all manner of produce and daily needs.

At one end of the bay, 2 km (1 mile) from the town, is the ferry jetty for services running east of Lombok to Sumbawa, the next island in the Lesser Sundas group.

EAT

Rinjani Lodge Restaurant

Guests enjoy spellbinding mountain views from tables and chairs or comfortable beanbags at this rustic restaurant. Both local and international dishes are on the menu. Favourites include *gado-gado*, creamy pasta, cashew-nut chicken and chocolate lava cake.

⊞ C4 🏠 Jalan Pariwisata, Senaru 🌐 rinjanilodge.com/restaurant

Ⓡ Ⓡ Ⓡ

Pringgasela

⚠C5 ☒From Sweta & Labuhan Lombok
ℹMataram; (0370) 632 723 or 634 800

The shady Pringgasela village lies in the cool, quiet foothills of Gunung Rinjani. Many villagers here are weavers, happy for visitors to watch. Outside many of the houses colourful textiles are displayed for sale. The patterns and hues, predominantly blacks and reds, are characteristic of Lombok.

In the hills south of Pringgasela is another craft centre, Loyok, Lombok's premier basketware, bamboo and palm-leaf handicraft village. The road from Loyok runs parallel to a fast-flowing stream that runs through beautiful forests and valleys.

Tetebatu

⚠C5 ☒From Mataram
ℹMataram; (0370) 632 723 or 634 800

A hill-station village, Tetebatu offers good views of Gunung Rinjani and has a relaxing ambience. The village itself is quite modest, but over an area running 3–4 km (2–3 miles) up the mountain slope there are a number of guesthouses, set among rice fields.

Pleasant walks are to be had in the mountain air, passing large-leaved tobacco plantations. One hike runs to a small river into which flows the Jeruk Manis Waterfall – the route is quite strenuous but can be tackled by fit, older children, as well as adults. Other walks lead to isolated villages and a tropical forest inhabited by monkeys. It is advisable to engage one of the guides who offer their services in the village.

Rembitan and Sade

⚠B6 ℹMataram; (0370) 632 723 or 634 800

The farming villages of Rembitan and Sade, which are approximately 3 km (2 miles) apart from one another, are both attractively set against the hillside. Despite the fact that many visitors stop here, and therefore sellers of souvenirs abound, Rembitan and Sade remain good places to catch a glimpse of traditional Sasak life, in which weaving textiles, growing rice and rearing goats and cattle are major occupations. A distinctive feature of the area is the *lumbung*, a bonnet-shaped rice barn. Once a symbol of Lombok, these barns are now less commonly seen. The walls of the thatch-roofed barns and houses are made of bamboo or palm-leaf ribs.

Gerupuk

⚠B6 ℹMataram; (0370) 632 723 or 634 800

The village of Gerupuk is situated on the edge of a

> Gerupuk is home to one of south Lombok's most popular surf breaks. In the bay, swells from the Indian Ocean build up and break on coral reefs, creating fine waves.

TEXTILES IN LOMBOK

Hand-woven textiles, of very high quality, are produced in Lombok using traditional backstrap looms. The villages that specialize in textile-weaving are Sukarara, Pringgasela, Rembitan and Sade. There is some larger-scale production around Mataram. In the villages, the entire process of cloth-making can be watched by visitors, from the boiling of barks and roots to make dyes, and the soaking of cotton threads, to the weaving of original patterns on the hand-operated loom. The villagers use only natural plants for the dyes. Yellow dye, for example, is made from an extract of turmeric root, while blue comes from the indigo plant. Roots and bark are pounded and boiled; the cotton threads are immersed for 24 hours, and, when dry, are arranged on the loom in the manner demanded by the pattern of the textile.

long bay. Villagers mostly live in simple reed huts and there is a mosque at the centre of the village. Gerupuk's main income, apart from fishing, comes from seaweed cultivation. The seaweed, which is used as an ingredient in food products for farm animals, grows on semi-submerged bamboo frames that are situated in the waters off the beach. After being harvested it can be seen drying in neat bundles along the roadside.

Gerupuk is home to one of south Lombok's most popular surf breaks. In the bay, swells from the Indian Ocean build up and break on coral reefs, creating fine waves. Surfers hire a small skiff for the short trip to

A sea of green rice fields and coconut trees in the village of Tetebatu

the break, and the journey itself gives breathtaking views of the nearby cliffs and rocky crags. The skiffs anchor a short distance from the break and await the surfers' return. The waves here are considered more user-friendly and forgiving than many of the others on this coast, where the sea can often be rough. They break on coral deep enough not to cause undue worry to board riders, unlike the shallow breaks and steep take-off points of Maui near Selong Blanak to the west. While the waves mostly break right, left breaks also peel off, although less regularly. The surf is at its best early in the morning before any wind gets up – usually before 9am – but even later in the day when crosswinds blow offshore, the waves are fine. Surfers from around the world come here and create an international community.

Sukarara

🅰 B5 🚌 From Sweta
ℹ Mataram; (0370) 632 723 or 634 800

Many people in Sukarara earn their living by weaving *songket* textiles *(p136)*. Large numbers of shops display and sell many varieties of local cloth. Village women will demonstrate their expertise with the loom and are willing to pose for photographs.

Penujak

🅰 B5 🚌 From Sweta
ℹ Mataram; (0370) 632 723 or 634 800

Along with Banyumulek *(p189)* and Masbagik, Penujak is one of Lombok's main pottery-producing villages, and perhaps the best place to see the process, which the villagers will explain. Traditionally, women made the pots by hand while the men marketed them. Now that export sales have led to increased output, men join in the production process. Each village produces its own distinct pottery, but all the designs are available in all three places.

↑ A villager creating a traditional pot in Penujak

EAT

Horizon at Ashtari

A Lombok landmark on a hilltop, Horizon Ashtari offers views of forest-clad hills. It serves Mediterranean dishes along with some local fare.

A B6 **□** Jalan Mawun Prabu, Kuta

KRNK

Juicy burgers, great cocktails, cheesy pizzas and great tunes: KRNK is the sort of place where casual dinners turn into raucous parties.

A B6 **□** Jalan Raya Kuta 5a, Kuta **W** krnk-lombok.com

Warung Flora

This friendly, family-run restaurant in an open-sided bamboo hut specializes in superb freshly caught fish. There are other local dishes on the menu too.

A B6 **□** Jalan Pariwisata Pantai Kuta, Kuta **C** (0878) 6530 0009

Bush Radio

Set in an old warehouse, this industrial-chic bistro serves home-baked sourdough bread, tasty salads and pizzas, accompanied by smoothies and fresh juices.

A B6 **□** Jalan Raya Kuta, Kuta **C** (0823) 3987 4778

Kuta

A B6 **□** From Sweta **i** Mataram; (0370) 632 723 or 634 800

Lombok's Kuta was originally most famous for its surf, for it is here that the island's mellow waters meet the powerful currents of the Indian Ocean, forming world-class surf breaks.

When Lombok's international airport opened at Praya in 2011, Kuta became an easily accessible destination. It now has a wide choice of accommodation and restaurants alongside its picture-postcard white-sand beach, making it an ideal base for exploring the cliffs, headlands and beaches of the rugged southern coastline, set against a backdrop of hills spotted with tobacco fields.

The 7-km- (4-mile-) long bay extends to the white sandy beach of Putri Nyale, which rests spectacularly beside a craggy limestone pinnacle on the shores of a crystal-blue lagoon. The beach is famous for the ancient Sasak legend of Princess Mandalika. The beautiful princess is said to have been strongly desired by six of the rival princes of Lombok, and each had threatened to attack her father's kingdom if their proposals of marriage were rejected. On a moonlit night, in allegiance to her father and for the wellbeing of her people, the princess publicly flung herself into the ocean from the hilltop on the east side of the beach, sacrificing herself so that no prince could have her. Once her body touched the water, it was transformed into many colourful sea worms – celebrated during the annual Bau Nyale Festival held here.

Tanjung Aan Beach

A B6 **□** 8 km (5 miles) east of Kuta

The almost impossibly beautiful, white-powder-sand beach of Tanjung Aan is famous for its surf breaks. When the tide is out, the bay turns into shallow pools of turquoise water. Tanjung

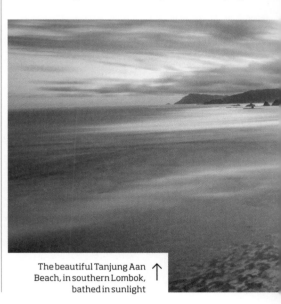

The beautiful Tanjung Aan Beach, in southern Lombok, bathed in sunlight ↑

BAU NYALE FESTIVAL

Every February or March, when the forces of the sea and moon coincide, masses of *nyale* – luminous sea worms – arrive and reproduce in the moonlight off Putri Nyale Beach. The *nyale* is considered a great delicacy. Hundreds of Sasak people assemble on the beach for an all-night feast, during which the worms are eaten grilled, fried or sometimes even raw.

Aan encompasses two bays: Aan to the west and Pedau to the east, separated by a rocky outcrop. The waters offer safe opportunities for swimming and snorkelling, but there can be a strong current on the eastern bay. Cafés on the pristine beach offer tables and sunbeds.

Check out Bukit Meresek, a hill at the western end of the bay with a lovely view at sunset, as well as Batu Payung – an extraordinary, towering, coastal landform on the eastern point with large, striking rock formations.

↑ A local fisherman untangling his net on Mawun Beach

Mawun Beach

B6 **10 km (6 miles) west of Kuta**

Though the approach to Mawun is down a long, pot-holed road, the serenity of the secluded beach is well worth it. Mawun is one of the most picturesque beaches in south Lombok. Here, a horseshoe-shaped crescent of white sand borders a perfect half-moon bay, sheltered by two massive headlands, all of which make the generally calm turquoise waters popular for swimming. However, when the swell is large enough, there are good right-hand and left-hand barrels for surfing. There are some large shade trees and small *warung* here serving simple local dishes; they also rent out sunbeds and umbrellas.

23
Bangko Bangko

🅰 A5 🚌 From Lembar
ℹ Mataram; (0370) 632 723
or 634 800

A popular place for fishing and surfing, Bangko Bangko lies at the end of a peninsula at the southwest extremity of Lombok. It can be reached only along a dirt road. The reward for this trip somewhat off the beaten track is the spectacular scenery.

Some surfers have named the area Desert Point. The waves that peel to the left off a coral shelf, before slamming into the base of the cliff face, provide great conditions for experienced riders. The unpredictable, often dangerous seas are good for game fishing. A fishing trip can be booked via tour operators in Lembar.

24
Selong Blanak

🅰 B6 ℹ Mataram; (0370) 632 723 or 634 800

Marked at each end by rocky promontories, Selong Blanak is a tranquil bay

with a fishing settlement and tourist accommodation and facilities. On the beach are multi-coloured outrigger canoes. There are also numerous little cafés, souvenir stands, surfboard rentals and ice cream vendors. Visitors to Selong Blanak Beach can often witness the magnificent sight of a large herd of water buffaloes being ushered along the sand from one grazing ground to another by a team of Sasak cowboys late in the afternoon.

Most people come to Selong Blanak to surf at the nearby Maui beach. The waves are exceptionally fast. Because of the steep take-offs and the fact that the waves here are ridden over very shallow coral, this is a place for very experienced surfers only.

25
Tanjung Luar

🅰 C5 ℹ Mataram; (0370) 632 723 or 634 800

The village of Tanjung Luar earns its living from the sea. It is a minor port – travellers from nearby islands land here by means of an inter-island taxi service which uses small outriggers. Many occupations to do with fishing and the sea are represented here and there is a busy fish market. Fishers return to port after spending several days afloat, and sell their catch beside the water's edge. It is possible to watch huge sharks being brought to shore. Contributing to the lively atmosphere are the salt-sellers, the children fishing off the main jetty, and the people giving their boats a new coat of paint.

A short walk from the fish market, lining the beachfront, live some Bugis communities, their wooden houses raised on stilts. Colourful Bugis schooners, with distinctive high prows, lie at anchor here.

For many people in Tanjung Luar, *cidomo* are the only form of transport. These are small

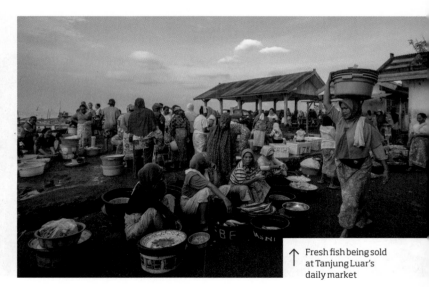

↑ Fresh fish being sold at Tanjung Luar's daily market

Sun setting over a fishing boat moored off the island of Gili Asahan ↑

Did You Know?

The small, idyllic Southwestern Gili Islands number at least a dozen in total.

horse-drawn buggies, brightly painted and often decorated with vivid red pompoms and tassels.

Banyumulek

A B5 **From Mataram**
Mataram; (0370) 632 723 or 634 800

This village of wooden huts with thatched roofs is a centre for the production of hand-made terracotta pots. Here, visitors can see how they are made and roam among the displays of pots, some decorated with textiles and rattan. Buyers of items too large to carry can have them shipped abroad if necessary.

About 3 km (2 miles) west of Banyumulek, an easy climb up Gunung Pengsong leads to a good view. From the Hindu shrine at the top, Bali's Gunung Agung and Lombok's Gunung Rinjani are visible in opposite directions. On one side the plain of Mataram stretches to the sea; on the other is an arc of rugged mountains.

Southwestern Gili Islands

A A5 **from Tembowong, Senggigi or Lembar**

Sprinkled off the north shore of Lombok's southwestern tip are the "Secret Gilis", two groups of tiny emerald islands. Gili Nanggu, Gili Genting and Gili Tangkong form part of the cluster close to Lembar, while Gili Gede, Gili Asahan and Gili Poh constitute a little archi-pelago further west, just off the coast near Pelangan.

While some of the islands are sparsely inhabited, others are not much more than rocky prominences. All have white-sand beaches, peppered with palm trees, cowrie shells and ghost crabs. Still relatively undeveloped, they offer a natural environment of idyllic beaches and abundant corals. Gili Gede (*gede* means "big") is the largest and best-known island off the Sekotong Peninsula, and it also has the widest selection of accommodation options, comprising a number of cottage-style hotels and homestays. There are no motorized vehicles. This is a working island; the villages are actively involved in pearl farming and fishing.

Gili Nanggu is very quiet, and perfect for diving, snorkelling or just relaxing, with just a few simple cottages on the beach and a restaurant. On Gili Asahan there is an eco-resort, several beach-bungalow hotels, a couple of restaurants and some excellent dive spots, such as Secret Garden, Sanking Point and Belongan, with its cluster of coral pinnacles.

A daily fastboat runs from Bali to Gili Gede and there are boat services from Tembowong Harbour, Senggigi and Lembar in Lombok to the other Southwestern Gili islands.

> **Still relatively undeveloped, the southwestern Gili Islands offer a natural environment of idyllic beaches and abundant corals.**

NEED TO KNOW

Food vendor stalls in the rain, Kuta, Bali

BEFORE
YOU GO

Things change, so plan ahead to make the most of your trip. Be prepared for all eventualities by considering the following points before you travel.

AT A GLANCE

CURRENCY
Indonesian
Rupiah (IDR)

AVERAGE DAILY SPEND

SAVE	SPEND	SPLURGE
Rp590,000	Rp1170,000	Rp3650,000

BOTTLED WATER	COFFEE	BEER	DINNER FOR TWO
Rp10,000	Rp30,000	Rp30,000	Rp700,000

ESSENTIAL PHRASES

Good morning	Selamat pagi
Goodbye	Selamat tinggal
Excuse me	Permisi
Thank you	Terima kasih
I don't understand	Saya tidak mengerti
Please	Silahkan

ELECTRICITY SUPPLY

Voltage is 220 volts, 50 Hz. Plugs and sockets are the European two-pronged variety.

Passports and Visas

For entry requirements, including visas, consult your nearest Indonesian embassy or check the **Indonesian Immigration** website. The citizens of 40 countries (including the USA, the UK, Australia and New Zealand) can apply for a Visa on Arrival (VOA), at Ngurah Rai Airport's arrival hall, which allows free entry for up to 30 days. The VOA can be extended for an additional 30 days for a fee.
Indonesian Immigration
W imigrasi.go.id

Government Advice

Now more than ever, it is important to consult your government's advice before travelling. The **UK Foreign and Commonwealth Office**, the **US State Department** and the **Australian Department of Foreign Affairs and Trade** offer the latest information on security, health and local regulations.
Australian Department of Foreign Affairs and Trade
W smartraveller.gov.au
UK Foreign and Commonwealth Office
W gov.uk/foreign-travel-advice
US State Department
W travel.state.gov

Customs Information

You can find information on the laws relating to goods and currency taken in or out of Indonesia on the **Directorate General of Customs and Excise** (DJBC) website. There are restrictions on the import and export of items made from endangered species, and on the export of antiquities and certain cultural objects.
Directorate General of Customs and Excise
W beacukai.go.id

Insurance

We recommend taking out a comprehensive insurance policy covering theft, loss of belongings, medical care, cancellation and delays, and read the small print carefully. Check that coverage includes medical evacuation: treatment of serious conditions often requires an emergency transfer to Singapore.

Vaccinations

For information regarding COVID-19 vaccination requirements, consult government advice.

Cholera, hepatitis A, typhoid and polio inoculations are recommended, and tetanus shots should be up to date.

If you have visited a country in the yellow-fever zone (some parts of Africa and South America) within six days prior to entering Indonesia, a vaccination certificate is required.

Dengue fever has been reported in Bali and Lombok, and malaria is a real risk in Lombok, so consult your doctor about preventive medication well before you begin your trip.

Money

Bali and Lombok use the Indonesian Rupiah (IDR) as their main currency. Many hotels quote rates in US dollars, but they are rarely accepted in practice. Credit and debit cards are broadly accepted, but contactless is rare and cash is still the main mode of payment.

Tips are always appreciated. Waitstaff, drivers and tour guides will expect 10–15 per cent.

Booking Accommodation

Bali and Lombok offer a huge range of accommodation, from cheap stays to luxury resorts. Online booking is available for nearly all hotels, but is not always reliable for those on the offshore islands, so it's worth double-checking by phone. Book well in advance during the peak seasons of July, August and Christmas, when accommodation costs rise.

Travellers with Specific Requirements

Bali and Lombok have a long way to go when it comes to accessibility. Wheelchair access is very rare, pavements are high and uneven, and public transport is inaccessible. The more up-market hotels and villas, however, are slowly becoming increasingly aware of the needs of disabled

travellers. **Bali Access Travel** lists accessible accommodation and transport companies, and organizes day tours. For more options, including longer tours, contact **Accessible Indonesia**.
Bali Access Travel
W baliaccesstravel.com
Accessible Indonesia
W accessibleindonesia.org

Language

The most widely spoken languages in Bali are Indonesian and Balinese, and in Lombok, Indonesian and Sasak. English is the main foreign language spoken.

Opening Hours

> **COVID-19** Increased rates of infection may result in temporary opening hours and/or closures. Always check ahead before visiting museums, attractions and hospitality venues.

Friday As Lombok is largely Muslim, most offices close between 11:30am and 2pm for prayer.
Weekends Most banks close at noon Sat.
Public holidays Banks and government offices close, but most shops and private businesses operate as normal.

PUBLIC HOLIDAYS

1 Jan	New Year's Day
7 Mar	Bali Hindu New Year
3 Apr	Isra Mi'raj
1 May	Labour Day
19 May	Waisak Day
1 Jun	Pancasila Day
5 Jun	Hari Raya Idul Fitri
6 Jun	Lebaran Holiday
12 Aug	Idul Adha
17 Aug	Independence Day
30 Aug	Islamic New Year
10 Nov	Prophet Muhammad's Birthday
25 Dec	Christmas Day

GETTING AROUND

Whether you are making a flying visit, or heading off on a lengthy adventure, discover how best to reach your destination.

AT A GLANCE

PUBLIC TRANSPORT COSTS

KUTA TO UBUD

Rp250,000

Metered taxi fare

KUTA TO UBUD

Rp60,000

Shuttle Bus

KUTA TO UBUD

Rp300,000

Car and Driver

Note: journey times can vary considerably according to traffic

SPEED LIMIT

TOLL ROAD

100 kp/h (62mph)

DUAL CARRIAGEWAYS

80 kp/h (50mph)

MAIN ROADS

60 kp/h (37mph)

URBAN AREAS

40 kp/h (25mph)

Arriving by Air

Flying to Bali

Bali's only airport is **Ngurah Rai International Airport**, situated 13 km (8 miles) south of Denpasar. It is often referred to as Denpasar International Airport. Major international airlines serving Denpasar include Garuda Indonesia (Indonesia's national carrier), Air Asia, Air New Zealand (seasonal), American Airlines, ANA, Cathay Pacific Airways, China Airlines, China Southern, Delta, Emirates, Eva Air, Jetstar, KLM, Korean Air, Lion Air, Malaysia Airlines, Philippine Airlines, Qatar Airways, Royal Brunei, Singapore Airlines, Thai Airways International, Virgin Australia and Xiamen Airlines.

There are frequent direct flights to Denpasar from Australia and some countries in East Asia, such as Singapore, Thailand and Japan. Carriers from other countries go no further than Jakarta, from where there are frequent Garuda Indonesia flights to Denpasar. Many travellers from Europe fly to Singapore, Bangkok or Kuala Lumpur, where they can catch regional budget airline flights to Denpasar. Carriers from Taiwan (China Airlines) and Hong Kong (Cathay Pacific Airways) stop in their own capital cities, from where travellers can connect to flights to Denpasar.
Ngurah Rai International Airport
W bali-airport.com

Flying to Lombok

Lombok's **Zainuddin Abdul Madjid Airport**, near Mataram, is mainly served by domestic flights from other parts of Indonesia. The easiest and fastest way to get from Bali to Lombok (and vice versa from Lombok to Bali) is by plane. Flight times from Bali's Ngurah Rai International Airport to Lombok's Zainuddin Abdul Madjid Airport take only around 25 minutes. SilkAir flies directly between Lombok and Singapore and Air Asia flies directly between Lombok and Kuala Lumpur. Garuda Indonesia has an international network of flights that serve Jakarta and Surabaya, from where you must connect to a domestic flight to Lombok.
Zainuddin Abdul Madjid Airport
W lombok-airport.co.id

GETTING TO AND FROM THE AIRPORT

Airport	Destination	Taxi Fare	Journey Time
Bali Airport	Kuta	Rp120,000	15 mins
	Seminyak	Rp150,000	25 mins
	Sanur	Rp175,000	25 mins
	Canggu	Rp300,000	40 mins
	Ubud	Rp350,000	60 mins
	Candi Dasa	Rp450,000	1 hr 40 mins
	Lovina	Rp600,000	1 hr 50 mins
	Amed	Rp 800,000	2 hrs 50 mins
Lombok Airport	Senggigi	Rp220,000	1 hr 20 mins
	Mataram	Rp160,000	50 mins
	Kuta	Rp90,000	30 mins
	Bangsal Harbour	Rp350,000	1 hr 30 mins

ROAD JOURNEY PLANNER

Plotting the main driving routes according to journey time, this map is a handy reference for travelling between Bali and Lombok's main destinations by car. The times given reflect the fastest and most direct routes available.

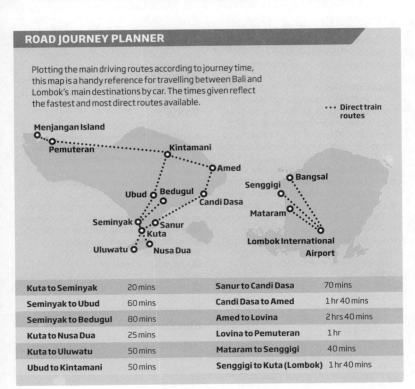

Kuta to Seminyak	20 mins	Sanur to Candi Dasa	70 mins
Seminyak to Ubud	60 mins	Candi Dasa to Amed	1 hr 40 mins
Seminyak to Bedugul	80 mins	Amed to Lovina	2 hrs 40 mins
Kuta to Nusa Dua	25 mins	Lovina to Pemuteran	1 hr
Kuta to Uluwatu	50 mins	Mataram to Senggigi	40 mins
Ubud to Kintamani	50 mins	Senggigi to Kuta (Lombok)	1 hr 40 mins

Local Transport

Public transport in Bali and Lombok is cheap, but not always convenient for visitors. Routes are designed to serve the needs of the local population rather than visitors, and services become scare after dark.

Buses

Buses operate long-distance inter-city and inter-island routes. The main ones are from Denpasar to Singaraja, Denpasar to Amlapura and Sweta to Labuhan Lombok. Fares (non-negotiable) are paid to the driver or the conductor. Tickets cannot be bought in advance except for inter-island trips.

The main terminals in South Bali are around Denpasar: at Batubulan in north Denpasar; at Kereneng in central Denpasar; and at Ubung in west Denpasar.

Bemos

Bemos are minivans that drive along pre-determined routes. Small *bemos* service a town while large *bemos* travel between towns, such as from Denpasar to Ubud or Kuta. Fares are low (less than Rp10,000 within a town and less than Rp20,000 between towns), but tourists are sometimes overcharged. Due to the price of tickets and the fact that *bemos* are often very hot and crowded, take a long time to travel short distances, and do not tend to adhere to set routes and times, they are generally not favoured by visitors or those on a tight itinerary.

Tourist Shuttles

Tourist shuttles – minivans or minibuses that travel between tourist destinations at regular intervals – are a very convenient way to get around Bali and Lombok. They are also a good place to meet other travellers, as they typically seat between eight and twenty people.

Several companies, such as **Perama**, run services between the major tourist destinations on a regular schedule at reasonable prices (fares range from Rp35,000 to Rp175,000). **Kura-Kura Bus** (fares from Rp20,000) is a Japanese-owned tourist shuttle bus service connecting the popular tourist areas of Kuta, Legian, Seminyak, Sanur, Ubud, Jimbaran and Nusa Dua. It is preferable to book tickets in advance.

Perama
w peramatour.com/transport/shuttle
Kura-Kura Bus
w kura2bus.com

Boats and Ferries

Although the islands of Bali and Lombok seem quite near to each other, the crossing is long and sometimes dangerous as the ocean between them can get very rough. Boat and ferry operators change constantly and it is a good idea to do some research on the ground for the ones that adhere to best safety practices.

The cheapest way to cross the Lombok Straits is by ferry. Ferries travel from Padang Bai in East Bali to Pelabuhan Lembar in Lombok at 60- to 90-minute intervals, but the crossing takes at least four hours, depending on conditions. It is worth getting to Padang Bai well in advance in order to board one of the newer (and more reputable) ferries. Tickets are purchased at the harbour. Seating is available in an air-conditioned saloon; however, this is not as pleasant as being on the deck.

There are multiple fast boat companies travelling between Bali and Lombok; Bali and Gili Air, Gili Trawangan and Gili Meno; Bali and Gili Gede; Bali and Nusa Lembongan; and Bali and Nusa Penida. Departures are from Benoa, Serangan, Padang Bai and Amed. Fast boats to Nusa Lembongan and Nusa Penida depart from Sanur. Prices are competitive but choose one that has a good reputation and guarantees you a seat – some companies overload their boats.

Day Cruises

Various companies operate cruises off Bali and Lombok. **Bali Hai** offers day cruises from Benoa Harbour to Lembongan, Nusa Penida and Nusa Ceningan islands. Cruise options include watersports activities, dolphin-watching trips and glass-bottomed catamarans for viewing coral reefs.
Bali Hai
w balihaicruises.com

Taxis

In South Bali and in Senggigi on Lombok, metered taxis can easily be flagged down in busy areas or ordered by phone or via an app. Taxis are much scarcer elsewhere, including major towns such as Ubud. Sometimes drivers will try to negotiate a flat fee, but it is usually cheaper to use the meter. It's best to avoid taxis where the driver refuses to use a meter. Reliable companies include **Blue Bird Taxi** and **Grab** whose drivers also speak good English.
Blue Bird Taxi
w bluebirdgroup.com
Grab
w grab.com/id

Private Transport in Bali and Lombok

Having your own transport opens up a range of exciting possibilities for travel in Bali and Lombok, not least the chance for unscheduled detours, spur-of-the-moment stops and forays off the beaten track. Traffic conditions are daunting for the uninitiated, however, so renting a car with a local driver (which can be done for around Rp900,000 per day) is often the best option.

Driving

If you plan on driving in Indonesia you must have an International Driving Permit, which is best obtained in your own country if you already have a valid driver's licence. If you have an accident when driving without a valid international licence and International Driving Permit, you will not be covered by your travel insurance policy – always carry both.

Car Rental

Self-drive cars are available in the main tourist areas where rental companies and tourist agencies rent cars at reasonable prices. The car rental company will deliver the car to you and pick it up at the end of the rental period. Always test-drive the car and check that it is in good working order before paying. You won't be allowed to take a rented car from Bali to Lombok or vice versa.

Parking

Parking in towns and at markets is supervised by a parking attendant who collects a small fee (generally Rp2,000–10,000 depending on the vehicle) and helps you get back onto the road.

Motorbikes

Motorbikes are widely available for rent, and can be particularly good for getting around in more isolated areas, especially in Nusa Penida and South Lombok where the roads are rough and potholed. Traffic conditions can be hazardous, however, so inexperienced riders should think twice before renting a bike. An International Driving Permit valid for motorbikes is required.

Helmets must be worn by law but the cheap ones provided by rental agencies offer little protection, so bring your own or buy a good one from a local shop, especially one with a face shield for protection from sun, rain, bugs and dust. Drive slowly and very carefully – accidents are increasingly common.

If you do not want to drive a motorbike yourself, you can hire an *ojek* (motorbike taxi) – these are more common in Lombok than Bali. They are best on quiet country roads but may be a bit precarious in the large towns. *Ojeks* do not have a meter so you need to agree a set price before you start your journey. If the operator doesn't provide you with a helmet do not get on the bike. You can book an *ojek* via the **Go-Jek** app.

Go-Jek

🔳 go-jek.com

Rules of the Road

Indonesians drive on the left-hand side of the road. At intersections where you are going straight ahead rather than turning, hazard lights should be used. Traffic regulations are often ignored on the mainland, and on the islands of Bali and Lombok: motorbikes overtake on either side; drivers pull out into traffic without looking, expecting you to avoid them; and vehicles regularly turn or change lanes without indicating. Right of way belongs to whoever is bigger or flashes their lights first. It is normal practice to sound the horn briefly before overtaking.

As Bali's pavements are scarce and narrow, pedestrian traffic flows onto the roads, and includes livestock, pushcarts, religious processions and cyclists going the wrong way. In Lombok, traffic is much lighter, but you must watch out for pony carts.

Driving just after dark is generally inadvisable because of poor visibility and, in particular, the inadequate lighting on bicycles and motorcycles. Drivers should watch out for piles of black sand on the road (dumped there for the next day's building activities).

Cycling

Cycling is a very enjoyable way to explore quieter areas of Bali and Lombok but care should be taken as potholes and other obstacles abound. Extreme caution must be exercised on busy roads, where bicycles are at the very bottom of the traffic hierarchy, especially in Bali. In Lombok the traffic is generally less chaotic throughout the island.

Plenty of bicycles are available for rent in all the tourist areas, but it's best to ask your accommodation to recommend a rental firm. Before you pay for one, make sure the wheels are properly aligned, the brakes work well and that there is a working light. Wear a helmet for extra safety, and try not to ride at night when roads are very poorly lit, or not lit at all.

Walking

Due to Bali and Lombok's lack of pavements and busy roads, it's not recommended to explore urban areas on foot. Head out to the islands' countryside, however, and it's a different story. Here, hikers trek through verdant ride paddies, tangled jungle and volcanic plains to secret waterfalls, ancient temples and soaring mountains. Favourite routes include the 4-km (2.5-mile) Campuhan Ridge Walk in Ubud (*p97*), the mountainous climb up Gunung Batur (*p120*) and strolling through the Tegallalang Rice Terraces (*p108*).

PRACTICAL
INFORMATION

A little local know-how goes a long way in Bali and Lombok. Here you will find all the essential advice and information you will need during your stay.

AT A GLANCE

EMERGENCY NUMBERS

AMBULANCE	FIRE
118	**113**

POLICE	RESCUE
110	**111**

TIME ZONE
GMT + 8
There is no daylight saving time period.

TAP WATER
It is not safe to drink the tap water in Bali and Lombok. Use bottled water or refill from hotel and restaurant dispensers.

WEBSITES AND APPS
Bali.com
Find out where to eat, sleep and play on this website *(www.bali.com)*.
Lombok Indonesia
An online guide to Lombok *(www.lombokindonesia.org)*.
Living in Indonesia
A guide for current and future expatriates *(www.expat.or.id)*.
Bali Tourism Board
Bali's official tourism board website *(www.balitourismboard.or.id)*.

Personal Security

It is important to exercise caution when visiting Indonesia. Violent crime is rare, but bag-snatchings and pickpocketing can occur in tourist areas. Be very careful with your belongings, and beware of motorbike-mounted snatch thieves. Report any theft to the English-speaking tourist police if you wish to make an insurance claim. Contact your embassy if you have your passport stolen, or in the event of a serious crime or accident.

Although people of all races and religions are welcome, Indonesia is a Muslim nation and all travellers should respect local religious customs and decency laws. Bali is majority Hindu, but many of the same rules apply on the island as elsewhere in the country.

All travellers, regardless of sexual orientation, should use discretion. Public displays of affection are generally frowned upon, and should be avoided. While homosexuality is legal, same-sex marriage is not. Despite this, it's unlikely that LGBTQ+ travellers will encounter any problems on their trip. Seminyak, South Bali and Ubud, in particular, have large LGBTQ+ communities and offer a number of welcoming venues. **Utopia Asia** has a comperehensive guide to Bali and Lombok's LGBTQ+ Scene.
Utopia Asia
🅦 utopia-asia.com

Health

Healthcare provision is generally poor in the islands' remote areas, though there are good – if expensive – private clinics in Bali, including the **International SOS Medical Centre**. It is, therefore, very important to have comprehensive medical cover included in your insurance policy. Check that coverage includes medical evacuation: treatment of serious conditions often requires an emergency transfer to Singapore.

For minor ailments, visit a pharmacy. Stomach upsets, caused by unfamiliar food and climate, and poor hygiene, are the commonest issue. Rest and rehydration are the main treatments; seek advice from a pharmacist or clinic if there is no improvement after a couple of days. Mosquitoes are a nuisance, especially in Lombok where malaria is prevalent, so cover up in the evenings and use repellent.

International SOS Medical Centre
🅦 internationalsos.co.id

Smoking, Alcohol and Drugs

Smoking is generally not allowed indoors in public places such as air-conditioned restaurants. Alcohol is widely available in tourist areas and, unlike in other Muslim nations, drinking is socially acceptable – though homebrew *arak* is sometimes dangerously tainted and should be avoided. It's not unusual for tourists to receive unsolicited offers of illegal drugs on the streets, especially in Kuta, Bali. Possession can result in lengthy prison sentences – or extortion by corrupt officials.

ID

Tourists are not legally required to carry ID, though it is advisable to carry at least a photocopy of some form of official identification, particularly when travelling outside of the main tourist areas. If you are stopped by the police and asked to present your passport, hand over the photocopy or ask to present the original document at the police station in the presence of other officers.

Local Customs

The Balinese will make visitors very welcome as long as they behave with due respect. Anger and confrontation, as well as public displays of private affection, are considered embarrassing to others and therefore rude. Intimacy is kept behind closed doors, especially in Lombok, which is majority Muslim. Even holding hands is viewed as unseemly; link arms with your partner instead. Overly revealing clothing is also frowned upon, so dress modestly.

There are several customs around the body. Avoid touching someone on the head, which is considered sacred. Pass things with your right hand, rather than your left hand as the left hand is considered unclean. Do not point at someone – beckon people by extending your hand and using a downward waving motion.

Visiting Sacred Sites

Visitors must follow strict rules when visiting Hindu temples and Muslim mosques. When entering a mosque, cover your arms and legs. Women should also cover their hair with a scarf. In Balinese temples, a waist sash and, in many places, a sarong, must be worn. These may be borrowed (or rented for a small charge) at temples that regularly accept tourists, but it is easy to buy your own almost anywhere. Note that food must not be brought into a temple as it clashes with offerings.

Certain people are prohibited from entering Hindu temples. This includes those who are currently menstruating or have an open wound – this relates to a prohibition on shedding blood in a temple – and people who are physically or mentally unwell.

Mobile Phones and Wi-Fi

Wi-Fi is ubiquitous in the islands' tourist areas, with nearly every hotel, restaurant and café providing a free connection. International GSM mobile phones usually have coverage, but confirm with your network before travelling to the islands. If you're planning on using your phone a lot, it might be cheaper to buy a pre-paid local SIM card, which are readily available from phone shops. You'll be asked for proof of ID and vendors will generally set up your new SIM card for you if you have an unlocked phone.

Post

Post offices are available in all the main tourist areas on the islands. Letters and postcards can take up to two weeks to reach destinations. It is possible to send parcels through post offices, but couriers such as DHL and UPS are faster and more reliable.

Taxes and Refunds

In Indonesia, a 10 per cent sales tax is usually included in the marked price of retail goods and services, though some hotels and high-end restaurants add it to the bill at the end, plus an 11 per cent service charge. No tax refunds are available for departing visitors.

INDEX

Page numbers in **bold** refer to main entries.

GLOSSARY

ARCHITECTURE

atap: palm-leaf thatched roof
bale: pavilion
candi bentar: split gate
gedong: enclosed pavilion
kori: roofed gate
kori agung: grand gate
kulkul: drum tower
meru: multitiered shrine
padmasana: tall shrine to the Supreme Deity
pelinggih: shrine, spirit house
pura: temple
puri: palace, house of nobility
rumah: house
wantilan: public pavilion with double roof
warung: coffee stall, small shop

ARTS AND CRAFTS

geringsing: warp- and weft-dyed textile, "double ikat"
ikat: warp resist-dyed textile
kayu: wood
lontar: type of palm; palm-leaf book
lukisan: painting
mas: gold
pande: metalsmith
paras: volcanic stone used for building and statuary
patung: statue
perak: silver
prada: gilt-painted cloth
songket: textile with supplementary weft thread, often gold or silver
tapel: mask
tenunan: weaving

MUSIC AND DANCE

arja: Balinese opera
baris: classical solo male dance
baris gede: a sacred dance for rows of male dancers
Barong: large sacred effigy danced by two men
belaganjur: processional percussion orchestra
gambuh: ancient court dance
gamelan: percussion orchestra
gangsa: bronze-keyed instrument
kebyar: vigorous style of gamelan music; vigorous solo dance
kendang: drum
keris: sacred wavy-bladed dagger
legong: classical dance for three females
prembon: mixed programme
Rangda: sacred demonic effigy, consort of the Barong
rejang: sacred dance for rows of female dancers
suling: bamboo flute
tari: dance

topeng: masked dance based on geneological tales
trompong: bronze instrument with 8 to 8 kettle gongs
wayang kulit: shadow puppet theatre
wayang wong: masked dance based on Hindu epics

DRESS

baju: shirt, dress
baju kaus: T-shirt
destar: head cloth for Balinese males
gelungan: ornate headdress
jilbab: head cloth for Muslim females
kain: cloth; long hip cloth, unsewn
kebaya: traditional jacket for females
peci: hat for Muslim males
sarong: sewn long hip cloth
selendang: ceremonial temple sash
sepatu: shoes

RELIGIONS AND COMMUNITY

banjar: village association
hari raya: any religious holiday
karya: work, especially collective ritual work
mesjid: mosque
odalan: temple festival
pedanda: high priest
pemangku: temple priest
penjor: festooned bamboo pole
pura dalem: temple of the netherworld
pura desa: village temple
pura puseh: temple of origins
sebel: taboo
sunat: Islamic ritual circumcision
tirta: holy water
yadnya: Hindu ritual (generic)

FOOD

air minum: drinking water
ayam: chicken
babi guling: roast pig
babi: pork
bakar: grilled
bebek tutu: smoked spicy duck
buah-buahan: fruit
cumi-cumi: squid
daging: meat
gado gado: vegetarian dish with peanut sauce
garam: salt
goreng: fried
gula: sugar
ikan laut: fish
jeruk nyepis: lime
jeruk: orange; citrus
kelapa: coconut
kopi: coffee
makan: eat
mie: noodles

minum: drink
nasi: food; rice; rice meal
pedas: hot (spicy)
pisang: banana
roti: bread
sambal: spicy condiment
sapi: beef
sate, sate lilit: small skewers of barbecued meat
susu: milk
teh: tea
telur: egg
udang: prawn, shrimp

NATURE AND LANDSCAPE

bukit: hill
burung: bird
danau: lake
gunung: mountain
hujan: rain
jalan: road
laut: sea
mata hari: sun
pantai: beach
pohon: tree
sawah: ricefield
subak: irrigation cooperative
sungai: river, stream
taman: garden, park
tanah: ground, earth, soil

TRAVEL AND TRANSPORT

bemo: public minibus
cidomo: rubber-tyred pony cart (in Lombok)
dokar: pony cart
jukung: outrigger sailing canoe
mobil: car
sepeda motor: motorcycle

MISCELLANEOUS

adat: customary law or tradition
bagus: good
baik: good
Bapak: polite term of address for a man
bayar: pay
cantik: pretty
dingin: cold
Ibu: polite term of address for a woman
mahal: expensive
murah: inexpensive
panas: hot, warm
pariwisata: tourism
puputan: suicidal fight-to-the-end
rokok: cigarette
sakit: hurt; sick
selamat jalan: farewell ("on your journey")
terima kasih: thank you
tidak: no, not
tidur: sleep
uang: money

ACKNOWLEDGMENTS

DK would like to thank the following for their contribution to the previous edition: Rachel Lovelock, Andy Barski, Albert Beaucourt, Bruce Carpenter, John Cooke, Jean Couteau, Diana Darling, Sarah Dougherty, Julia Goh, Lorca Lueras, Zoe Ross, Tim Stuart, Tony Tilford

The publisher would like to thank the following for their kind permission to reproduce their photographs:

Key: a-above; b-below/bottom; c-centre; f-far; l-left; r-right; t-top

123RF.com: balinature 88cl; Florian Blümm 152bl; iferol 159t; ivohausner 105tr; Ronnachai Limpakdeesavasd 11cr; Aleksandar Todorovic 66bl, 74tr.

4Corners: Jürgen Ritterbach 122–3b.

Alamy Stock Photo: 24BY36 36b; age fotostock / Frederic Soreau 76t; Terry Allen 117; Konstantin Andreev 84–5b, 108tl; ART Collection 54t; Art Directors & TRIP 52cl, 52clb; Putu Artana 53tl; Arterra Picture Library 24cr, 121clb, 164b; Artokoloro Quint Lox Limited 55cra; Asia File 34–5t; Romina Bayer 174br; Sabena Jane Blackbird 129tr; Paul Brown 22tl; pavlos christoforou 20cl; Chronicle 56br; Sue Clark 129br; Thomas Cockrem 42t, 55tl, 73br, 178bl; Cultura Creative (RF) 47b; Leila Cutler 132clb; David Buch Photography 39cl; Chris Deeney 41t; Design Pics Inc 45cl; Marius Dobilas 86tr; Brad Downs 27tl; Eagle Visions Photography / Craig Lovell 22–3t, 161t; Peter Eastland 20bl, 73tr, 132bl; Martyn Evans 37br; Dima Fadeev 28bl; Michele Falzone 50bl, 66–7, 108–9b; Christine Gates 150br; Sioen Gérard 127tr; GoSeeFoto 78br; Hagen Production 41cl; Vince Harris 165tr; Hemis 13br; Horizon Images / Motion 70–1t, 86–7b; KC Hunter 100–101; imageBROKER 139tr; INTERFOTO 55bl; Ivoha 43cr; Jango / Stockimo 103cla; JHMimaging 37tl; John Warburton-Lee Photography 106cl; Jon Arnold Images Ltd 137br, 185cla; Kenishirotie 38br; John Kershaw 45br; Ronnachai Limpakdeesavasd 121br; Christoph Lischetzki 30cl, 106bl; LOOK Die Bildagentur der Fotografen GmbH 26tr, 100cra, 184b; Edmund Lowe 20t, 110–11; MARKA 104tl; Stefano Politi Markovina 185br; master2 180bl; mauritius images GmbH 98bl; Annette Maya 153br; Aliaksandr Mazurkevich 24t, 40br; Military History Collection 56–7t, 57clb; Igor Mojzes 39crb; Denis Moskvinov 47cl, 52cr; nikjvt 59tr; Roberto Nistri 95br; Nokuro 143tr; Angela Nott 95cla; Agung Parameswara 130–31b; Carlos Peñalba 172–3; Photononstop 153crb; Peter Pinnock 149bc; Christian Platzer 26tl; Grant Rooney Premium 23tl; Juergen Ritterbach 105br; robertharding 41br, 43cla, 49cla, 55cb, 140t, 158br; RooM the Agency 27tr, 172clb; Reynaldo Santa 150tr; Norbert Scanella 156–7t; Peter Schickert 28cr; Leonid Serebrennikov 43tr, 107t, 136–7t; Simon Pierce 12t; David South 157br; Constantin Stanciu 40tl; Wayan Sulendra 131tr; Mulawardi Sutanto 44tl; Ariyani Tedjo 34tl, 35cl; travelib Indonesia 46bl; Yuliya Trukhan 141b; Dray van Beeck 37c; Mykola Velychko 24cl; Nitish Waila 12–13b; Rob Walls 100bl; Christine

Wehrmeier 27ca; Michel & Gabrielle Therin-Weise 154cra; Karin De Winter 163br; Jan Wlodarczyk 10ca, 154clb; Poelzer Wolfgang 138b.

AWL Images: Marco Bottigelli 18tl, 112–13; Michele Falzone 2–3, 69t.

Bridgeman Images: Christie's Images / Willem Gerard Hofker © DACS 2018 *Phantastic Bali, poster advertising the Bali Hotel, Indonesia* 56tl; Pictures from History 55tr, 55cr, 99br.

Courtesy of Ashtari Lombok: 24br.

Depositphotos Inc: luckybusiness 10clb; tashka2000 48–9t.

Dreamstime.com: Amadeustx 124bl; Christophe Amerijckx 13t; John Anderson 162t; Arttikstockphotography 42clb; Kairi Aun 116clb; Kitchner Bain 95tr; Florian Blümm 153cb; Shariff Che\' Lah 125tl; Christophefaugere 175br; Tomas Ciernik 160b; Cmeili87 33c; Cocosbounty 83br, 102b, 165bc; Dvrcan 98–9t; Feathercollector 149cra; Aqnus Febriyant 74b; Oliver Förstner 123tr; Elizaveta Galitskaya 94–5b; Galjan 116b, 119t; Bradley Hay 157cl; Idmanjoe 118cl; Dmitry Islentyev 51ca; Joyfull 80–81t; Elena Krutikova 43b; Leoraduga 174–5t; Lev Levin 119bc; Edmund Lowe 35crb, 49br, 50–51t; Denis Moskvinov 4; Christian Nilsen 175tc; Jon Chica Parada 181t; Tomas Pavlasek 44–5b; Marek Poplawski 154–5; Anthony Prince 187tl; Ruengrit 30t; Oktobernardi Salam 23tr, 148; Softlightsea 19, 168–9; Somma695 68bl; Nikolai Sorokin 164clb; Hiroshi Tateishi 125tr; Telnyawka 159cr; Matthew Train 6–7; Venemama 126t; Visualism Studio 36tr; Andra Wayan 133tr; Weltreisendertj 123cr; Wonderful Nature 84tl; Tayfun Sertan Yaman 149crb.

Getty Images: AFP / Jewel Samad 59cr, / Sonny Tumbelaka 53tr, / STR 59br; Bettmann 56clb; Raung Binaia 142–3b; Larry Burrows 58bc; Culture Club 54crb; Fadil Aziz / Alcibbum Photography 189t; Michele Falzone 18cb, 134, 144–5; John Florea 57tr; Isa Foltin 167tr; IN2 Focus Media 188b; Moment / @ Didier Marti 78–79t; Justin Ong 53br; Agung Parameswara 52cla; raditya 178–9t; James R.D. Scott 177tr; simonlong 58–9t; Terence Spencer 58tl; Maria Swärd 186–7b; Andrew TB Tan 22–3ca; torstenvelden 120–11t; Maya Vidon- White 59clb; Alfian Widiantono 172cra, 182–3b.

iStockphoto.com: AlenaPaulus 176cra; asiafoto 131tl; Bicho_raro 88–9t; Valery Bocman 121crb; Em Campos 48–9b; CEphoto, Uwe Aranas 81br; ChanwitOhm 45tr; Csondy 10–11b; Andrey Danilovich 8–9; dislentev 83t; DKart 17, 90–91; enviromantic 34b; ErmakovaElena 190–91; Goddard_Photography 131cla; ifew 32b; joakimbkk 32tl; johan10 57bc; jon11 46–7t; KellyOla 34cra; KitHamilton 149clb; LadyBird89 8cl; laughingmango 63clb; mahos 96t; mahroch 28t; manjik 16, 62–3; master2 69cra, 72–3b; MelanieMaya 30clb; miralex 119br, 128bl; Myslitel 33br; NicoElNino 11br; Nikada 97cra; PrinPrince 172bl; raung 8cla, 33tl; RibeirodosSantos 60–61; Iuliia Serova 66tr; Shrekton 13cr; steffie82 183tr; swissmediavision 38–9t; Aleh Varanishcha 30br.

Mowie's: 26–7ca.

Picfair.com: Theodora 53cl.

Shutterstock: EPA / Made Nagi 53cr; Elizaveta Galitckaia 54bl; Guitar photographer 166-67b; R.M. Nunes 11t; Tebha Workspace 53bl.

Robert Harding Picture Library: G & M Therin-Weise 125cla, 154bc.

SuperStock: age fotostock / Carol Buchanan 95tl, / Jan Wlodarczyk 20cr, / Leonid Serebrennikov 12clb, / Manfred Gottschalk 51br; Axiom Photographic / Design Pics / Peter Langer 28crb; Cultura Limited 176–7b; imageBROKER / Moritz Wolf 52cra; Mauritius 149cl.

Ubud Writers & Readers Festival: Anggara Mahendra 52crb.

Front Flap:
123RF.com: Aleksandar Todorovic cb; **Alamy Stock Photo:** Dima Fadeev cra; Jon Arnold Images Ltd cla; **Getty Images:** James R.D. Scott bl; **iStockphoto.com:** DKart br; **SuperStock:** Cultura Limited tc.

Cover images:
Front and Spine: **Getty Images:** Moment / Nora Carol Photography.
Back: **Alamy Stock Photo:** Michele Falzone cla; **Getty Images:** Moment / Nora Carol Photography b; **Dreamstime.com:** Denis Moskvinov c; Tawatchai Prakobkit tr.

For further information see: www.dkimages.com

Illustrators: Anuar Bin Abdul Rahim, Denis Chai Kah Yune, Chang Huai-Yan, Choong Fook San, Koon Wai Leong, Lee Yoke Ling, Poo Lee Ming, Thomas Sui, Peggy Tan, Yeap Kok Chien.

This edition updated by

Contributor Marco Ferrarese
Senior Editor Alison McGill
Senior Designers Ben Hinks, Vinita Venugopal
Project Editors Parnika Bagla, Rebecca Flynn
Art Editor Bandana Paul
Editor Anuroop Sanwalia
Picture Research Administrator
Vagisha Pushp
Picture Research Manager Taiyaba Khatoon
Publishing Assistant Halima Mohammed
Jacket Designer Jordan Lambley
Senior Cartographer Subhashree Bharati
Cartography Manager Suresh Kumar
Senior DTP Designer Tanveer Zaidi
Senior Production Editor Jason Little
Senior Production Controller Samantha Cross
Deputy Managing Editor Beverly Smart
Managing Editors Shikha Kulkarni,
Hollie Teague
Senior Managing Art Editor
Priyanka Thakur
Art Director Maxine Pedliham
Publishing Director Georgina Dee

First edition 2001

Published in Great Britain by Dorling Kindersley Limited, DK, One Embassy Gardens, 8 Viaduct Gardens, London SW11 7BW, UK

The authorised representative in the EEA is Dorling Kindersley Verlag GmbH. Arnulfstr. 124, 80636 Munich, Germany

Published in the United States by DK Publishing, 1745 Broadway, 20th Floor, New York, NY 10019, USA

Copyright © 2001, 2022 Dorling Kindersley Limited
A Penguin Random House Company
22 23 24 25 10 9 8 7 6 5 4 3 2 1

A CIP catalog record for this book is available from the British Library.

A catalog record for this book is available from the Library of Congress.

ISSN: 1542 1554
ISBN: 978 0 2414 7394 8

Printed and bound in Malaysia.

www.dk.com

MIX
Paper from
responsible sources
FSC
www.fsc.org **FSC™ C018179**

This book was made with Forest Stewardship Council ™ certified paper – one small step in DK's commitment to a sustainable future. For more information go to www.dk.com/our-green-pledge

---

A NOTE FROM DK EYEWITNESS
The rapid rate at which the world is changing is constantly keeping the DK Eyewitness team on our toes. While we've worked hard to ensure that this edition of Bali and Lombok is accurate and up-to-date, we know that opening hours alter, standards shift, prices fluctuate, places close and new ones pop up in their stead. So, if you notice we've got something wrong or left something out, we want to hear about it. Please get in touch at travelguides@dk.com